AN IN-DEPTH STUDY OF P

Come
LET US WORSHIP

ELIZABETH BAGWELL FICKEN

Front Cover Design: Michal Rudolph
Back Cover Design: Jeannine Klingbeil

*Special thanks to Randy McKinion, my seminary professor who suggested
a women's Bible study on Psalms and who encouraged my Hebrew language
project in the Psalms; and special thanks to his wife, April McKinion, for
being my friend, ministry partner, and encourager during seminary.*

*One thing I have desired of the Lord, that will I seek:
that I may dwell in the house of the Lord all the days of my life,
to behold the beauty of the Lord, and to inquire in His temple. Psalm 27:4* [NKJ]

ISBN-10: 0-9905933-3-9
ISBN-13: 978-0-9905933-3-1

Table of Contents

Table of Contents (cont.)

Introduction

Dear Friends,

We are about to begin a study of an amazing collection of poems and prayers. It's fascinating to think about God inspiring each of the authors and preserving the songs of their hearts, so that we too could pray and praise our Lord along with these saints who have gone before us. The Psalms contain many of our most well-known and well-loved Scriptures. We turn to them so often for comfort and to express the emotions of our souls. The Psalms also challenge us to live godly lives, to worship and adore our great and glorious God, to make the right choices in the midst of overwhelming trials, and to always trust the Lord. The Psalms lead us to keep our priorities straight by telling us to meditate on God's word and to worship Him as King. These two key themes will be seen throughout our study.

There are one hundred and fifty chapters of this beautiful book! I would love to study each one of them with you, because I know that each psalm is of eternal value. But, for now, the Lord has led me to select one psalm per day for most of our lessons. Sometimes, we will study several psalms together, because they just go hand in hand. It was so hard to choose less than 150 psalms to study! I felt like I was standing in the midst of a flower shop, with vase after vase filled with the most beautiful specimens grown in the gardens on display for my choosing. I wanted to include every single one!

Well, let's enjoy the bouquet that the Lord has created for us. We'll see some familiar favorites, as well as some psalms that you may have never noticed before. Some are short, some are long, some are bright and full of praise, others express heartbreak and suffering. But all together, they prompt us to turn to the Lord and see that He is with us every moment of our lives, in control, faithful, loving, wise and worthy of all our devotion. The psalms remind us to look forward to the day in which He will reign on the earth and we will worship Him as our great and glorious King. While we wait for Him, and when we see Him.... let us worship the King.

Do You Know Jesus?

This is the most important question in this study. Please notice that I didn't ask you if you know about Jesus. But do you know Him, personally?

The Bible teaches that God loves you.
"For God so loved the world . . . that He gave His one and only son that whoever believes in Him will not perish, but have eternal life." John 3:16 *ESV*

And it teaches that God wants you to know Him personally.
"Now this is eternal life, that men may know Him, the only true God, and Jesus Christ whom He has sent." John 17:3 *ESV*

But . . . people are separated from God by their sin.
"Your sinful acts have alienated you from your God" Isaiah 59:2 *NET*

Sin causes us to miss the very best for our life.
"Jesus said, 'I came that you might have life and have it to the full." John 10:10 *NIV*

Sin causes us to face death and judgment.
"The wages of sin is death." Romans 3:32 *NAS*
"Those who do not know God . . . will pay the penalty of eternal destruction away from the presence of the Lord." 2 Thessalonians 1:8-9 *NAS*

But there is a solution! Jesus Christ died and conquered death for you! We deserve death and judgment, but Jesus took upon Himself the punishment for our sins, so that we could have a personal relationship with God.
"For there is only one God and one Mediator who can reconcile God and humanity-- the man Christ Jesus. He gave his life to purchase freedom for everyone." 1 Timothy 2:5-6 *NLT*

It's not enough just to know this. Each of us by faith must receive Jesus Christ if we want to know God personally.
"To all who have received Him—those who believe in His name—He has given the right to become God's children." John 1:12 *NET*
"For it is by grace you have been saved, through faith—and this not from yourselves, it is the gift of God." Ephesians 2:8 *NIV*

The ABC's of faith involve:
Acknowledging your need—admitting you have sinned and desiring to turn from sin. (1 John 1:8-9)
Believing Jesus Christ died in your place and rose again to be your Savior—providing forgiveness for your sins. (1 Corinthians 15:3-4:17)
Choosing to invite Christ to direct your life. (Romans 10:9)

Your desire to have a personal relationship with God can be expressed through a simple prayer like this: "Dear Lord, I want to know You personally. Thank you for sending Jesus who died in my place and rose again to be my Savior. Please forgive my sins. I am willing, with your help, to turn from my sins. Come into my life and lead me. Amen."

*For illustrations and more information, go to **KnowHimPersonally.com***

Reading and Responding to the Psalms

In other studies, I begin each lesson with a reminder for you to turn to the Lord in prayer and to trust the Holy Spirit to teach you the Word of the Lord. That specific reminder is not written out for you in this book, but the concept is still in place! Every lesson begins with instructions to read the psalm being studied and personally respond. This is to be a time of turning to the Lord and depending on Him to communicate His message to you. Please take time to record your reflections, your questions, or your prayers in response to what you have read. This is an exercise in reading, meditating upon, and contemplating God's Word. You might even call it journaling! I am aware that not everyone enjoys writing their thoughts down. So, I'll share my experience and some questions you can consider if you need a little direction in this process.

My own experience in journaling has developed over the years. I used to laugh at the idea and just kept notes in my Bible rather than in a notebook of any kind. But the habit of writing thoughts down came early on when I first learned to have quiet times. I have several little books about "how to have a quiet time" and they all suggest that you use a notebook to record thoughts, reactions, and prayers to the Bible reading. The following questions are suggested to prompt our thoughts about the Scripture:

> *Is there any example for me to follow?*
> *Is there any command for me to obey?*
> *Is there any error for me to avoid?*
> *Is there any sin for me to forsake?*
> *Is there any promise for me to claim?*
> *Is there any new thought about God Himself?*

The six basic journalism questions are also helpful and easy to remember: Who? What? When? Where? Why? How? Just ask these questions regarding the text. Who is it about? What is being said? When - are there time elements involved? Where are we to go, not go, where do we want to be? Why should God answer? Why should I behave this way? How am I to live? How am I to trust, how do I wait?

In a nine month period of time, I read through the Book of Psalms twice and both times I did just what I'm asking you to do. I read the psalm and wrote down my response. I reacted to the truths of the psalm with excitement, confusion, wonder, or submission depending on the content of the psalm. Sometimes, I just summarized what I understood the psalm to be saying.

I hope you will take the time to experience this part of our time in Psalms. It will allow you to personally interact with the Lord and "talk" with Him about His Word.

Helpful Hints

If you are new to in-depth Bible study. You will need a Bible. Please feel free to use the version of your choice. There are many translations. If you are using a Catholic Bible or a Jewish Old Testament it will be helpful for you to also use a modern version of the Bible which includes the Old and New Testament.

I recommend the following versions which are available for free at online Bible study websites, in smartphone and tablet apps (see recommendations on the next page), or for purchase in Christian bookstores. They are usually referred to by the letters in parentheses.

New King James Version (NKJV)   New American Standard Version (NASB)
New International Version (NIV)   Holman Christian Standard Bible (HCSB)
English Standard Version (ESV)

This study was written using multiple translations. I have found that I can gain understanding of the meaning of verses by reading other versions of the same passage. Two other popular Bibles are *The Message* and the New Living Translation (NLT); these are both wonderful versions for comparative reading, but are not as appropriate for in-depth study.

Planning time for your lesson. Set aside a specific amount of time to work on the lesson. One lesson may take 30-40 minutes depending on your familiarity with the Scriptures. You may want to do the lessons in shorter increments of time, depending on your schedule and personal preferences. I find that I absorb, retain, and apply the message of the Scriptures better when I am not rushed.

Please begin your study time with prayer. Ask the Holy Spirit to give you understanding of God's Word, as it is promised that He will do according to 1 Corinthians 2:12-13: "Now we have received, not the spirit of the world, but the Spirit who is from God, that we might know the things freely given to us by God, which things we also speak, not in words taught by human wisdom, but in those taught by the Spirit, combining spiritual thoughts with spiritual words." I have given you a reminder at the beginning of each lesson.

Observation, interpretation, and application. The Scripture readings, activities, cross-references and word definitions are all placed in the order which is most appropriate to your study. It is best to follow this order if you can, rather than skipping steps or setting steps aside to be completed at a different time. The order follows the inductive study process: observation (what the Scripture says), interpretation (what the author intended, what the Scripture means) and application (what difference the Scripture makes in your life). You will be doing the research, cross-referencing and summarization of the truths of each passage. When you finish a study of a passage, you will have gleaned more understanding on your own than you will find in some commentaries!

Looking up Hebrew word definitions. One of the activities included to help you understand the correct interpretation of the scripture is discovering and considering the definition of a word in its original language. Please make sure that you look up the definition of the word in its original language, not the definition of the English word. You will be given a prompt like this:

Meditate: Strong's #1897
Hebrew word:
Hebrew definition:

There are several ways you can look up the words given.

- You can google the Strong's reference number (Strong's 1897) and your web browser will give you links to the definition.
- You can go to an online Bible study website (recommendations below) and use their free reference materials. Look for "study" tabs, "lexicons" (this is what Hebrew and Greek word dictionaries are called), "concordances" and "original language" tools. There are search boxes where you can type in the Strong's reference number. Use H before the number for Hebrew words (H1897).

    studylight.org   blueletterbible.com   searchgodsword.org

    Suggested resources, described on page xxx, are also available at these websites if you want to do more research on your own.
- You can download free Bible study apps for your smartphone and/or tablet. I use **MySword** which allows me to go to a passage and click on the Strong's reference number next to the word. Try a few different ones and see what you like best.
- You may have some great resources on your own bookshelves! Enjoy using books like: *Strong's Exhaustive Concordance* and *The Complete Word Study Dictionary* by Spiros Zhodiates.

If you have trouble, it would be better to skip the exercise rather than filling in the English definition.

It's about your head and your heart. My hope is that you will read portions of Scripture and gain understanding of what is being communicated through them so that you can consider how to apply the truth of God's Word to your life. I have tried to make the study "user-friendly" and I promise that I don't ask trick questions. I do want to make you think hard sometimes though! I hope you won't get overwhelmed. Do what you can, a little bit at a time. The reward of knowing our holy God through His recorded word far outweighs the time and effort of study.

Prayer requests and praises. You will find pages at the end of this workbook which provide prompts from Scriptures for your prayers as well as a place for you to write out a personal prayer request . If you are studying with a group, it would be helpful to reflect on your personal prayer request before sharing it with the group. Keep your requests brief and personal. This page is also a place to record the prayer requests of others.

The Book of Psalms

"Blessed is the man..."! What an exciting beginning to the book of Psalms! Who doesn't want to be blessed by the Lord? Who doesn't want to be happy? The true way to find happiness is laid out before us in the psalms. As we read and study one psalm after another, and consider not only what the individual psalm says but what the book of Psalms communicates to us as a whole, we will find out what brings true happiness, joy, and delight.

Flowers are an earthly blessing from the Lord that bring me happiness. I've begun to think of each psalm as a beautiful flower, with the book of Psalms containing many varieties, colors, shapes, and scents. Some are small and delicate, others larger with bright, bold colors. Some flowers have one exquisite bloom while others have multiple miniature blossoms. We will see great variety in the psalms, and will enjoy their unique contribution to the bouquet of our study one by one. Almost everyone has a favorite flower, and a favorite psalm. If yours wasn't picked for this particular bouquet, you'll still have a chance to enjoy its beauty as we go along!

We're going to start at the beginning, then look at one psalm after another, based on the order that the compiler of this great book created under divine inspiration. We'll see that the final author had a reason for arranging the psalms in this particular order. In between the psalms we're studying, there will be a section entitled "Arranging the Flowers" in which I will briefly describe the psalms we are not studying and how they relate or connect to the psalms around them.

Let's go ahead and look at how we know that someone put it all together on purpose.
Turn to Psalm 42. What heading is given at this point in the Psalms?

How does the previous psalm end? Write out the verse from Psalm 41:13.

Now turn to Psalm 73. What heading is given here?

How does the previous psalm end? Write out the verse from Psalm 72:18-19.

Turn to Psalm 90. What heading do you find?

Are you already looking at the ending of the previous psalm? Write out the verse from Psalm 89:52.

Book Four of the Psalms is a very short one! Turn to Psalm 107. What heading is given here?

What is the conclusion to Book Four, in Psalm 106:48?

Finally, turn to Psalm 146. The last four psalms of the Psalter create an extended doxology, praising the Lord, just as Books One, Two, Three, and Four did. Look at the first lines of Psalms 146, 147, 148, 149, and 150. What refrain is repeated in each of these psalms and all the way through the very last one?

You've just seen the grand finale, the great conclusion, and most important point of the book of Psalms! As we study the psalms together, we will see that the psalms are ordered in such a way as to lead us to think correctly about our God and to respond to Him according to who He is. He is worthy of our praise and worship!

The first two Psalms are crucial to our perspective of all that follow, so we will study them as the introduction to the book of Psalms in this lesson and the next.

Psalm One

Please read Psalm 1.

 *Following each first reading of the Psalm, please take time to record your reflections, your questions, or your prayers in response to what you have read. This is an exercise in reading, meditating upon, and contemplating God's Word.*

Respond with your reflections, questions, prayers or praise.

_____

_____

_____

_____

This psalm presents clear word pictures that contrast godly lives versus ungodly lives. Let's list these contrasts side by side.

The Blessed Man   **The Wicked Man**

The key to man's blessedness is found in verse 2. What makes a man happy?

There are three words that we should make sure that we understand. Please look up the following words in a Hebrew lexicon for word definitions. (I've given you more information about searching for word definitions on page 6.)

Law: Strong's #8451
Hebrew word:
Hebrew definition:

Meditate: Strong's #1897
Hebrew word:
Hebrew definition:

Delight: Strong's #2656
Hebrew word:
Hebrew definition:

When you think of the "law" of the Lord, what comes to mind? What books of the Bible contain the law? Did you learn in your research that the first five books of the Bible are called the "Torah" and that the word essentially means "teaching" or "instruction"? This concept helps us understand how Genesis, Exodus, Leviticus, Numbers, and Deuteronomy are called the "Law"; they are the words of the Lord that have been recorded for our instruction. These are probably the books that the psalmist was referring to in verse 2.

Do you take great delight in the books of Genesis, Exodus, Leviticus, Numbers and Deuteronomy?

At our present point on the eternal time line, we are privileged to have not only the Torah, but also the Prophets, the Proverbs, the Psalms, the Gospels and the Epistles as the written revelation of the Lord in which we may delight. Throughout our study we will see that the Psalms refer to the teachings from the rest of Scripture and they are quoted as Scripture in the New Testament.

Our delight in the law of the Lord will lead us to take action such as is described in verse 2. How often does the blessed man meditate on God's word? What are practical ways to meditate on God's word?

Oh, our lives are full of so much noise that it can be very hard to meditate, to ponder, to think about the words of the Lord. Let's take the opportunity right now to meditate on this very verse.

Write out Psalm 1:2.

Now read it aloud, slowly and softly.

Now repeat it phrase by phrase.

Choose one of the words from this verse and think about what it means. Record your thoughts.

Finally, restate this verse as a prayer.

That time of stillness and meditation before the Lord considering His word brought peace and quiet to my soul. I need to do that more often. One of the things I love about studying God's word is that it does prompt me to meditate, to think about, and to ponder His truths.

The first Psalm inspires us to meditate on the Word of God and live according to its teachings rather than any counsel of wicked men or counsel of the world. It is placed here as the introductory psalm to the whole collection so that we will realize as we read the rest of the psalms that the proper response to the law, the Torah, the instruction, is worship of the Lord.

Psalm Two

In this lesson we will continue with our introduction to the book of Psalms as given to us through Psalms 1 and 2. Remember, there are themes in these two psalms which will be repeated and progress until the very last note of praise in Psalm 150.

Please read Psalm 2.

Respond with your reflections, questions, prayers or praise.

_____

_____

_____

_____

What key word from Psalm 1 is found in the last phrase of Psalm 2:12? To whom does this word apply?

This is a royal psalm and a messianic psalm. It gives us a heavenly perspective of rebellious rulers on earth, the Lord's plan for the reign of His Anointed, and the right response to the King.

This Psalm is one complete, concise unit. It is easy to outline with four parts. Look at each section and answer the following questions.
Psalm 2:1-3: What's wrong with the world?

Psalm 2:4-6: What's right in heaven?

Psalm 2:7-9: Who will rule the earth?

Psalm 2:10-12: What will your response be?

Let's find out exactly who "the Lord's Anointed" is, because this Psalm describes His reign, and what the correct response to Him should be.

Please look up the following word:
Anointed: Strong's #4899
Hebrew word:
Hebrew definition:

*So who is the Lord's Anointed in Psalm 2? We have the full revelation of Scripture that interprets the meaning of mashiach in this verse for us. The book of Daniel gives the clearest indication in the Old Testament that **mashiach** is a special eschatological (end times) figure. He is not just an historical king of Israel. Chapter 9 records the message Daniel received from the angel Gabriel regarding the "latter days," which explained an incredible vision Daniel had received earlier.*

Daniel 9:25-26 says: "So you are to know and discern that from the issuing of a decree to restore and rebuild Jerusalem until Messiah (mashiach) the Prince there will be seven weeks and sixty-two weeks; it will be built again, with plaza and moat, even in times of distress. Then after the sixty-two weeks the Messiah (mashiach) will be cut off and have nothing, and the people of the prince who is to come will destroy the city and the sanctuary. And its end will come with a flood; even to the end there will be war; desolations are determined." In these verses, the Messiah appears and then is "cut off".

When we look to the New Testament, we come to understand the exact identity of the Messiah and what it meant for Him to be "cut off." Psalm 2 is quoted or referred to eighteen times from the Gospels to the book of Revelation.

Read Acts 4:23-27. (Peter and John have just been released from prison.)
What verses from Psalm 2 do they quote?

Who do they interpret as the ones who are in rebellion against the Lord and His Anointed?

Who are the kings of the earth gathered against? How is He described?

Please look up the following word (remember to look for the Greek definition):

Christ: Strong's #5547 (root word: #5548)
Greek word:
Greek definition:

The Messiah is Jesus, the Christ, who appeared on the earth, but then "was cut off" – He was rejected and crucified.

> "We have, in these first three verses [of Psalm 2], a description of the hatred of human nature against the Christ of God." – Charles Haddon Spurgeon

Psalm 2 gives us two important descriptions of the Lord's Anointed.

Who is He according to Psalm 2:6?

Who is He according to Psalm 2:7?

The Lord God, Yahweh, has placed His Son on the throne to rule over all the nations, even to the ends of the earth. And we see in the conclusion of this psalm that the only appropriate response is to worship the Lord, and seek refuge in Him through His Son, Jesus Christ.

Psalm 1 declares the blessing of the Lord upon the man who meditates on His word, and Psalm 2 declares the blessing of the Lord upon those who put their trust in the coming Messiah. Together these psalms serve as introductions to the rest of the book of Psalms, setting the stage for us to consider what makes one happy: living according to the word of the Lord, serving the Lord with reverence and worship, and trusting in the Messiah who is to come.

As we study through the rest of these inspired prayers, let's keep this perspective in mind. The Word of God and the Son of God, Jesus Christ the King, are to be the passion and pursuit of our lives from which we will receive all blessings. There is no thing and no one greater than these.

Arranging the Flowers

Psalms 3 — 7

I must admit that before beginning this study on the book of Psalms, I never wondered why the Psalms were in the particular order that they are. But I've learned that someone did have a plan. It's fascinating and I'll try to share a little with you as we transition from one psalm to another. There are words, themes, and situations which connect the psalms. It is probably unusual to you to think of reading the Psalms in context with one another, but when you do, you will see a tremendous truth.

God's plan for the ages is laid out before us. One day, God will place His Anointed King – Jesus Christ– on the throne to rule over the entire earth. The Psalms show us how to trust and obey God until Jesus comes as King; they give us David as an example of one who trusted God faithfully through all circumstances; they prophesy of the life, death, and resurrection of Christ; they describe what kind of King the Anointed One will be, and what His kingdom will be like; and the Psalms show us how to worship Him as Kings of Kings forever.

Psalm 3 begins: "a Psalm of David, when he fled from Absalom his son." Psalm 7 begins: "a Shiggaion of David, which he sang to the LORD concerning Cush, a Benjamite." These two psalms both appear to have been written during the time in David's life when Absalom was rebelling against him. Cush was the messenger who came to tell David that his son Absalom was dead. (See 2 Sam. 15:2 and 2 Sam. 18) Psalms 3, 4, 5, 6 and 7 all reflect a time in David's life when he was facing many enemies and looking to the Lord for safety. While each of these psalms has specific truths that they relate on their own, they also fit together as a group during this time of David's life and they demonstrate the life of one who was seeking refuge in the Lord, just as Psalm 2:12 advised all to do for blessing.

Psalm 7 closes this particular section of David's life, and ends with "I will give thanks to the Lord according to His righteousness and will sing praise to the name of the Lord Most High." (Ps 7:17) This statement almost seems as if it doesn't fit with the whole of Psalm 7. But, it sets the stage for the next psalm which is one of great praise to our glorious Lord.

Psalm Eight

"O Lord, our Lord, how majestic is Your name in all the earth!" Psalm 8:1 Does this sound familiar? Do you know a song with these words? I expect that this Psalm is a favorite of many of you. It stands out in our bouquet as an exquisite bloom. For all who rejoice in the Lord, for all who are amazed at His creation, for all who are humbled at His knowledge of them, this psalm expresses adoration and exaltation.

Please read Psalm 8.

Respond with your reflections, questions, prayers or praise.

_____

_____

_____

_____

It's possible to become so familiar with certain Scriptures that we miss the magnitude they convey and we may fail to revere our Lord in the manner in which He is worthy. Because of this, it is very important to observe the very first words out of David's mouth.

What does David say in verse 1 and repeat in verse 9?

Look up the following words in a concordance, word study dictionary, or lexicon as well as a Bible dictionary or Bible encyclopedia and record what you learn. These resources are available on Bible study websites and apps.

LORD: Strong's #3068
Hebrew word:
Hebrew definition:

Lord: Strong's #113
Hebrew word:
Hebrew definition:

Name: Strong's #8034
Hebrew word:
Hebrew definition:

The concept of the name of the Lord is more than a title; it is the idea of the Lord's reputation and character, of all that He has revealed of Himself to mankind. The first verse is repeated as the last verse of this psalm, and indicates that the majesty of the name of the Lord, the splendor and transcendence of His very being, is the central theme upon which the whole psalm rests. With an understanding of God's majesty and splendor, everything else in the world is put into proper perspective.

In nine short lines, this psalm answers the most important questions of mankind: Who is God? Who am I? Why am I here? After the death and resurrection of Christ, believers in the early church came to understand that this psalm also answers a fourth critical question for our lives: Who is Jesus? We will study this passage to discover the answers to these questions for ourselves.

Who is God according to this psalm? List the attributes and actions that describe Him in verses 1-4.

Who is man according to this psalm? Describe what you learn from verses 4-5.

The vastness of outer space and the knowledge that God created it all caused David to ask, "What is man...?" This phrase is found in the Hebrew only two other times, both in the book of Job. The question David asks is very similar to the question that Job asked in the midst of his despair when he said: "I despise my life; I would not live forever. Let me alone; my days have no meaning. **What is man** *that you make so much of him, that you give him so much attention, that you examine him every morning and test him every moment?" (Job 7:16-18) As David considers the greatness and power of the Lord, he is humbled before Him, even to a sense of despair which caused him perhaps to echo the words of Job. It is truly inconceivable that humans have any significance before the Creator of the universe. But the revelation of God's word, recorded in Genesis, gave David the words with which to respond to his question.*

Summarize the truths from Genesis 1:26-27 which are repeated in Psalm 8:4-8.

These truths give us the answer to the question: Why am I here? You've just read God's plan in Genesis 1:26-27, now read Genesis 1:28. What is Adam commanded to do?

Based on Genesis 1:28 and Psalm 8:6-8, what is the purpose of man?

In response to the incredible truths upon which David has just reflected, in verse 9 he declares once again his praise to God, repeating verse 1. Do you realize that you must always relate your own significance to that of God, remembering that God alone is sovereign and glorious? Reverence for the name of the Lord, for His splendor and majesty, is the foundation for the correct perspective of our lives and as much a purpose for our lives as is being fruitful, multiplying and subduing the earth. This psalm is a beautiful song of praise, recognizing the Lord as Creator of the world and of our lives. If only all men would always remember who God is, and who they are in relation to him. But they do not.

Sometime after receiving their high calling to be fruitful and multiply, and to subdue the earth, Adam and Eve sinned against God and forever changed the course of the world. Their sin has impacted every man and woman ever born, and while we all have the same high calling as they did, we fall far short of the Lord's purpose in our lives. Because of their first sin and because of our own sins, God sent Jesus into the world. The writer of Hebrews looks at Psalm 8 and sees Jesus as the one who truly fulfills the role given to Adam and to us.

When we understand Psalm 8 as explained in Hebrews 2:5-9, we will understand one final very important question for our lives: Who is Jesus?

Please read Hebrews 2:6-9. Who is Jesus according to this passage?

According to Hebrews 2:7 and 9, how is Jesus crowned with glory and honor?

Did you see any mention of death in Psalm 8? No. Please read the title of Psalm 9 now. What does it say? (If you are not using the New International version, you'll have to do a little more research. Either refer to the NIV or look up *muth-labben*, Strong's #4192.)

The rest of the book of Hebrews explains that Jesus' death served as a substitute for our death and served as the perfect sacrifice required for the removal of sin. Just as the last line of Psalm 7 prepared us for the song of praise sung in Psalm 8, so the title of Psalm 9 enables us to see Jesus in Psalm 8, as it refers to "The Death of the Son."

It was Jesus, the perfect man, who fulfilled the high calling given to Adam and the rest of mankind. He therefore is crowned with glory and honor. At Christ's return, the rest of Psalm 8:6 will be fulfilled, and all things will be in subjection under His feet.

Do you know who God is? Do you know who you are? Do you know why you are here? Do you know who Jesus is? What are your answers to these questions, based on your study today? How does this impact your life?

God is the sovereign Creator. We are made in His image. We have received dignity and honor from Him. Jesus is the perfect man who died on our behalf and He is crowned with glory and honor. Because God's grace gives us forgiveness through the death of His Perfect Son, we can praise the Lord even as David did, saying: O Lord, our Lord, how majestic is your name in all the earth."

Arranging the Flowers

These psalms are no less inspired, no less beautiful, no less eternally important! It's so hard not to spend a day on each one. We've already mentioned the critical importance of the placement and title of Psalm 9. Here are a few glimpses of the majesty of the Lord and a relationship with Him from Psalms 9 – 14.

Psalm 9

"I will give thanks to the LORD with all my heart; I will tell of all Your wonders.

I will be glad and exult in You; I will sing praise to Your name, O Most High."

Psalm 9:1 [NAS]

David says: "I will... I will... I will.... I will..." give thanks and praise the Lord. In keeping with the idea that the heading of this psalm and Hebrews 2:6-9 points out that Jesus Christ is the Son of Man in Psalm 8, who will perfectly rule the earth, Psalm 9 has as its theme the eternal kingship of God. The Lord will abide forever, His throne will be in Zion, and the wicked will be judged.

Psalm 10

"Why do you stand far off? Why do you hide yourself in the day of trouble?"

Psalm 10:1 [NIV]

Now David says where are you Lord? Why aren't you showing your power and justice? These questions confound us everyday when we see the actions of the wicked and their prideful scorn of God. This psalm gives us the Lord's perspective of the wicked: they are prideful, devising plots, boasting, cursing, and spurning the Lord, rather than honoring Him and submitting to Him. In the end, David is comforted as he anticipates the coming kingdom of the Lord, saying: "The Lord is King forever; the nations will perish from His land." (Psalm 10:16)

Psalm 11

"For the LORD is righteous, He loves righteousness;

the upright will behold His face."

Psalm 11:7 NAS

Troubles for David continue, and while he is tempted to flee to some mountain hideaway, instead he determines to find his refuge in the Lord. He asks: "What can the righteous do?" during times of suffering. The answer is given in verses 4-7: the righteous know who the Lord is, that He reigns, that He tests, that He judges, and that in the end the righteous will behold His face.

Psalm 12

"'Because of the devastation of the afflicted, because of the groaning of the needy,

now I will arise,' says the LORD; 'I will set him in the safety for which he longs.'"

Psalm 12:5 NAS

"Help, Lord!" There are so many days when we too experience troubles and call on the Lord. The previous psalms have shown us to anticipate His coming kingdom and judgment of the wicked, but this psalm shows us that the Lord provides comfort to us today. The Lord speaks and His words are "pure words; as silver tried in a furnace on the earth, refined seven times." The Lord will keep His word and He will keep and preserve the righteous. (Psalm 12:5-7)

Psalm 13

"How long, O LORD? Will You forget me forever?

How long will You hide Your face from me?"

Psalm 13:1 NAS

There are days, times, and seasons when we feel like the Lord is not with us. David expresses his soul's anguish in the silence of God. How long will this trial continue? He can only pray and request that the Lord – His God – will answer him. But while he is waiting, he will trust in the faithful, loyal love of God. He will rejoice in the deliverance which comes from the Lord alone, and he will sing to Him because of His goodness to him.

Psalm 14

"The LORD has looked down from heaven upon the sons of men

to see if there are any who understand, who seek after God."

Psalm 14:2 NAS

This psalm continues as those before it, describing the actions of those who do not submit to God, who commit acts of wickedness, who, thinking that God will not judge them say "there is no God." In contrast to the foolish, the "workers of iniquity", are "the righteous generation" and God is with them. The actions of the wicked once again prompt David to long for the coming salvation and kingdom of God. Anticipation of the presence of the Lord prompts the question asked in Psalm 15.

Psalm Fifteen

While previous psalms stated that the wicked will not stand in the assembly of the righteous, the godly were exhorted to seek refuge in God and promised that they would see God. This psalm brings into focus the desire of the godly to be in God's presence and describes the life of a righteous person. How should we live if we want to enjoy the presence of the Lord? Let's see what the inspired word of God tells us.

Please read Psalm 15. It will be helpful for you to read this in a few different translations.

Respond with your reflections, questions, prayers or praise.

_____

_____

_____

_____

Let's pause to try to grasp the description of the Lord's presence. How is the dwelling place of the Lord described in the following verses?

Psalm 2:6

Psalm 3:4

Psalm 5:7

Psalm 11:4

Psalm 15:1

Do you see one word repeated in each of these verses? It describes the place of the Lord because it is the very nature of the Lord.

Please look up the following word:
Holy: Strong's #6944
Hebrew word:
Hebrew definition:

Throughout the book of Leviticus, the Lord tells Moses to tell the priests and the people: "You shall be holy for I am holy." The holiness of the Lord is seen in that He Himself is set apart and separate from all of His creation. He is a being that is like none other; the only way to approach Him is in the manner which He describes. In Leviticus, the Israelites are given specific laws so that they will live lives set apart, separated from all other religions and people groups, and be a nation belonging to the Lord. But this psalm is not a list of ceremonial regulations and laws. It shows that holiness must be found in our hearts before it is found in our hands.

Describe the one who will be accepted in the presence of the Lord based on the two categories given below.

Goodness in action: (vs. 2, 4)   **Absence of evil: (vs. 3, 5)**

"The psalmist is not so much giving rules as painting a portrait of the kind of man who can remain in God's presence." [1]

How can we be blameless, righteous and truthful? This is not our nature at birth. We need a new nature. We must be cleansed from our sins. And what can wash away our sins? Nothing but the blood of Jesus!

Read Hebrews 10:10-14. What is the difference between the daily sacrifices of the priests and the sacrifice of the body of Christ?

Read Hebrews 10:19-22. What can we enter and to whom can we draw near? How?

Please read Psalm 15 again. Let's look more closely at the life that is described here.

Does Psalm 15:2 refer to the internal life or external life, or both? Explain any correlation between the three descriptions given.

How does Psalm 15:3 relate to the previous verse?

Psalm 15:4 describes the way a righteous man regards and responds to others, depending on whether they are wicked or righteous. Look back at Psalm 1:1-3; 4-6 for a reminder of a similar perspective. In your own words, summarize Psalm 15:4.

The last phrase in Psalm 15:4 is strange and hard to understand in any translation, even in the original Hebrew! I've come across two very probable interpretations. It may mean that the righteous person keeps their word (their oath), even when it becomes inconvenient, difficult, or painful to do so. Or it may mean that it is the duty of the righteous man to see that people do not get away with wrongdoing.

One way to translate this phrase is: "he has sworn to bring calamity and does not change it." [2] The vile person referred to in the first part of the verse should be held accountable for his actions. If this psalm refers to the one who is acceptable to God, then it is possible that this is a description of the only One who ever lived a blameless life in complete obedience to the laws of the Lord. Jesus Christ, the Anointed One, has sworn to judge those who have done evil (John 5:28-30). He will not change His oath.

Lastly, Psalm 15:5 describes the way that the righteous man handles his money. What do the cross-references below say that help us understand the following statements in Psalm 15:5?
"who lends his money without usury (interest)" Psalm 15:5a
Leviticus 25:35-37

Deuteronomy 23:19-20

"and does not accept a bribe against the innocent." Psalm 15:5b
Deuteronomy 16:18-20

Based on these verses, lending was to be a way to help a fellow Israelite, not be a means of increasing one's own wealth. Greed must be put away. And bribery perverted justice, even as it does today.

Please read Psalm 15 once more.

It is clear from this psalm that external actions come from internal character. If you have been cleansed by the blood of Christ, are you living like it? Is there anything in this psalm that the Lord has convicted you of?

What is the comforting promise to those who live a righteous life?

The psalms that we have spent time with so far set the foundation for the rest of our study. Each and every psalm in this book is based on faith in our unseen God, His true word, His present help, and His coming kingdom. We've seen that we will be blessed if we meditate on and obey the teaching of the Lord; we will be blessed if we submit to Him and anticipate His coming kingdom. We've seen that knowing Who God is gives us the proper perspective for who we are, and we've seen that to live in the presence of the Lord we must be holy as He is holy. And we have seen that Jesus Christ gave His perfect life as a sacrifice for us so that we might be cleansed and made holy.

Please respond to the Lord by praying through Psalm 16, which you will find is a declaration of wholehearted trust and steadfast faith in the Lord.

> You make known to me the path of life;
> In Your presence there is fullness of joy;
> At Your right hand are pleasures forevermore.
> Psalm 16:11 ᴱˢⱽ

Psalm Seventeen

How am I supposed to pray? I'm sure you've asked yourself and maybe others that question at some point in your life. While each psalm is a communication to the Lord, there are actually only five that are entitled "A Prayer" – Psalm 17, 86, 90, 102, and 142. In each of these, except for Psalm 90 which was written by Moses, the prayer comes from a time of dangerous situations and the writer cries out to God for deliverance. Psalm 17 is the prayer of an innocent person under extreme pressure.

At the end of the previous lesson, you prayed Psalm 16 as a declaration of trust. One author has said that "somewhere in the shadows of the psalms of trust trouble is lurking."[1] Psalm 16 and Psalm 17 are very closely related, and we may be seeing the danger that David mentioned in Psalm 16:1, 8, 10 more clearly expressed in Psalm 17. In the midst of his trouble, he prays well. Let's learn from his example.

Please read Psalm 17.

Respond with your reflections, questions, prayers or praise.

_____

_____

_____

_____

David makes three requests of the Lord with three supporting reasons for his requests.

What is his specific request in verse 1?

What reason does he give the Lord for responding to him in verses 2-5?

What are his specific requests in verse 6-8?

What reasons are woven into his requests in verses 6-8?

What is he experiencing according to verses 9-12 that prompts him to pray this way?

What is his specific request in verse 13-14?

In response to his request, what does he anticipate from the Lord according to verse 15?

If you view this psalm as a three-step plan for prayer, how would you describe those three steps?

> David would not have been a man after God's own heart if he had not been a man of prayer. He was a master in the sacred art of supplication. [2]

That gives us an overview of this Psalm. David presented reasons for God to answer his prayer, not because God needed to be persuaded to answer, but because the reasons prompted David to think about what he was asking for and to pray according to God's character and His promises.

David based his first request on his own innocence (verses 1-5). What does Isaiah 59:1-2 say that would help us understand why this reason is so critical?

One of the most important things that we can do when we begin to pray is to examine ourselves: our hearts, our motives, and our behaviors. We must be aware of whether or not we are approaching God rightly. David was claiming innocence in regards to the wrongs of which he had been charged by his enemies. He wanted God to vindicate him.

How can you base your prayers on your own innocence? We can, because, as we have seen in our study of Psalm 15, Jesus Christ has made the way for us to enter the Most Holy Place and be in the presence of our Holy God. But we must continue to examine our lives and confess the sins that we commit from day to day.

What does 1 John 1:9 say?

Please take time now to prepare yourself for prayer to the Lord. Do a little self-examination. Can you claim innocence as David did in verses 1-5? Have you been disobedient to the Lord, selfish, or neglected your God-given responsibilities? Have you wronged another person? Confess your sin to the Lord, and ask forgiveness from Him. Be reconciled to Him and to anyone else you may have sinned against.

David based his second request upon the character of God. Once again, read Psalm 17:6-8. What does he ask God to show him?

Please look up the definition for the following word:
Loving-kindness: Strong's #2617
Hebrew word:
Hebrew definition:

This word is so important in the whole Bible, and especially important in the Psalms. It occurs in 127 verses in 54 psalms. It is translated in several different ways: loving-kindness, love, mercy, steadfast love, loyal love, and faithfulness.

Turn for a moment to Psalm 136 – this word is in the repeated refrain in all 26 verses.
What is the refrain?

How did they know this? Look at the following verses in which God made covenants with Israel and with David. What did He promise? (*Chesed* is translated as mercy in NKJV and love in NIV)
Deuteronomy 7:9

2 Samuel 7:15

While we are looking at David's request based on the character of God, we need to see that he echoed two Songs of Moses as he prayed. David knew the character of God because he knew the written word of God.

What similarities do you see between the following Scriptures?

Exodus 15:11-13   **Psalm 17:6-8**   **Deut. 32:10-12**

_____   _____   _____

_____   _____   _____

_____   _____   _____

_____   _____   _____

From the book of Psalms, we learn that divine chesed saves people from disaster or oppressors. We are constantly surrounded by the threats of natural disasters, hostile enemies, and our own fleshly weaknesses. We turn to God to plead for Him to save us according to His chesed and we realize that God's faithful, loyal love is the only thing that protects us from disaster. We must, however, discover His loving-kindness, His faithfulness, at each new crisis. And while we can be assured that He will see us through the trials, the pain of the trial is rarely fully removed.

How have you experienced the loving-kindness of the Lord? Are you facing a trial and need His faithfulness to be demonstrated to you in a new way? Make your request known to Him, even as David did in Psalm 17:6-8.

I mentioned previously that there were close connections between Psalm 16 and 17. They are not only found in the trials that David was facing, but in the prophecy that was made in both of them. In the New Testament, Peter tells us that the Scripture in Psalm 16:10 was fulfilled in Christ.

Read Psalm 16:8-10 and Psalm 17:15. ("Awake" is a metaphor for the resurrection of the body.)

What do you learn about these two passages of Scripture from Acts 2:24-32?

Because Jesus Christ was raised from the dead, we too who believe in Him can be awakened to eternal life after death. This is the ultimate answer to all of our prayers.

Jesus said to her, "I am the resurrection and the life;
he who believes in Me shall live even if he dies,
and everyone who lives and believes in Me shall never die.
Do you believe this?"
John 11:25 NAS

Psalm Eighteen

We are about to encounter the first of several very long songs in this book of prayers, songs, and poetry. Only Psalm 73 and 119 are longer! This is a passionate song of a victorious warrior - a song of thanksgiving, a song of triumph, a song of the Anointed King. It appropriately follows the previous psalm of prayer for deliverance from enemies. It has been called a "gargantuan testimony to the way the Lord delivered from attack." [1] *It is a song of worship to the Lord and a song of witness to the people. The Lord loves to hear the praises of His people and He is worthy of many words of adoration and exaltation!*

Please read Psalm 18.

Respond with your reflections, questions, prayers or praise.

_____

_____

_____

_____

Briefly, with just a phrase if possible, describe the idea in each of the following sections of this psalm:

The title:

Verses 1-3:

Verses 4-6:

Verses 7-15:

Verses 16-19:

Verses 20-24:

Verses 25-29:

Verses 30-36:

Verses 37-42:

Verses 43-45:

Verses 46-50:

> The word "rock" here has reference to the fact that in times of danger a lofty rock would be sought as a place of safety, or that men would fly to it to escape from their enemies. Such rocks abound in Palestine; and by the fact that they are elevated and difficult of access, or by the fact that those who fled to them could find shelter behind their projecting crags, or by the fact that they could find security in their deep and dark caverns, they became places of refuge in times of danger; and protection was often found there when it could not be found in the plains below. [2]

> The word "horn" is often used metaphorically to signify strength and honor, because horns are the chief weapons and ornaments of the animals which possess them; hence, they are also used as a type of victory. [3]

This psalm is recorded in its entirety in 2 Samuel 22. Hmmm. If the Lord inspired the authors to record it twice, maybe we should read it twice. Please turn to 2 Samuel 22 and read the entire chapter. Worship the Lord for Who He is and what He can do to strengthen you.

This psalm describes many ways that the Lord is our refuge. List the ways that David describes the Lord as "*my* _____". (Psalm 18:1-6, 18, 46)

This psalm also describes God's deliverance with magnificent, poetic imagery which is based upon God's appearance at Mt. Sinai and during the time of Joshua and the judges.

What are the similarities between Psalm 18:7-15 and Exodus 19:16–19?

> David has in his mind's eye the glorious manifestations of God in Egypt, at Sinai, and on different occasions to Joshua and the judges; and he considers that his own case exhibits the same glory of power and goodness, and that, therefore, he may accommodate the descriptions of former displays of the divine majesty into his own hymn of praise. [4]

This psalm can give us great comfort and hope for deliverance out of our own trials. Why did the Lord deliver David, according to verses 16-24? (Notice that it specifically answers the prayer of Psalm 17.)

There is a further description of the character of God found in verses 25-29. What can we be assured of?

This reminds me of a "trustworthy saying" found in 2 Timothy 2:11-13. What can we be assured of according to these verses?

The statements of Psalm 18 are applicable to those who, as Psalm 1 and 2 established, delight in the law of the Lord and seek refuge in Him. And the statements of 2 Timothy 2 are applicable to those who have found refuge – salvation – in Jesus Christ as their Savior.

Each section of this psalm is rich with truth and encouragement, but I think verses 30-36 may be my favorite. What is most meaningful to you in this passage?

The song begins to come to an end in verses 37-42 with David's review of how he overcame his enemies by the strength of the Lord which he has been praising throughout the psalm. Then in verses 43-45 we see that the king is made ruler over all nations. David as king is a portrait of the Messiah as King over all the nations.

What is the conclusion to this great song of victory in verses 46-50? What does David proclaim?

Throughout the psalms, David praises the Lord as his rock, or calls out to Him to be His rock and refuge. How has the Lord been your rock?

Psalm Nineteen

This psalm – a song – moves from one grand theme to another. First the Lord is praised for His glory that is seen in creation. Looking up at a vast blue sky, countless clouds, a glorious sunrise…the heavens during the day prompt us to consider that they are a reflection of God's infinite, perfect, creative being. Nature shows us the Lord, but even more perfectly does His word reveal His character, His ways, His power, His plans.

The second half of the psalm directs our attention to the specific revelation of God through "Torah" – His word. Psalm 1, 19, and 119 are called Torah psalms because they emphasize the importance of knowing God's will through His word. The psalmist then, reflecting on the perfect word of the Lord, examines himself and prays that he will live according to it, in a manner acceptable to the Lord.

Please read Psalm 19.

Respond with your reflections, questions, prayers or praise.

_____

_____

_____

_____

Psalm 19:1 is written in the Hebrew using a poetic device called "chiasm." It was a way in which the writer would draw attention to a key theme. He would use words or phrases in one order, then reverse the order of the words or phrases. The middle of the verse or poem would therefore become the central focus. Chiasm is usually noted by using letters:

A

    B

    B'

A'

In the Hebrew, Psalm 19:1 is written:

(A) The heavens are declaring

(B) the glory of God

(B') the work of His hands

(A') is announced by the expanse.

With this understanding, what is the key point of this verse?

What are the very first words of the Torah? Record Genesis 1:1.

What do we learn about creation from Romans 1:20?

What are some of your favorite works of God's hands? How has God been revealed to you through His creation?

Do you think David might have been reading Genesis and reflecting on its truths when he composed this song? We've already seen that his composition in Psalm 8 was based on the creation of man as recorded in Genesis 3.

What was the king instructed to do in Deuteronomy 17:18-20?

What was Joshua instructed to do in Joshua 1:8?

And what makes a man happy, blessed, according to Psalm 1:2? (I hope you remember this!)

Why copy it, read it, meditate on it? What does the word of God do for us? David declared this in beautiful poetry in verses 7-11. List below the description of the word of God in each verse given, and the impact that it has on our souls.

I asked you earlier what some of your favorite works of God's hands are. Now, consider what some of your favorite words of God are.

What Scripture has revived your soul?

What Scripture gives you wisdom?

What Scripture brings joy to your heart?

David used many different words to describe the written word of God. But what phrase did David repeat throughout his declaration? Why is this important?

Let's look at the six different words used to describe the word of the Lord. They are more than synonyms. Look up the following words and their Hebrew definitions. Feel free to research further with a Bible dictionary.

Law: Strong's #8451
Hebrew word:
Hebrew definition:
(look back at pg.12 and summarize what you learned)

Statutes: Strong's #5715
Hebrew word:
Hebrew definition:

Precepts: Strong's #6490
Hebrew word:
Hebrew definition:

Commands: Strong's #4687
Hebrew word:
Hebrew definition:

Fear: Strong's #3374
Hebrew word:
Hebrew definition:

Ordinances: Strong's #4941
Hebrew word:
Hebrew definition:

> "The root meaning of Torah is 'instruction.' It has to do with everything God has revealed or says. Our best equivalent would be *Scriptures* or *the Word of God*. *Statutes* literally is "testimony." It means an aspect of truth attested by God himself, perhaps with the idea of this being a reminder. *Precepts* together with the word *commands*, which comes next, means 'orders,' indicating the precision and authority with which God addresses us. *Fear* is not strictly a synonym for law, though it is used as such. It describes the Scripture by the effect they produce in those who respond to the revelation. The last verses of the psalm are an example of this godly fear or reverence. The final noun, *ordinances*, means 'judgments' or 'verdicts', that is the divine evaluation of our thoughts and actions. [1]

With these words, David considers God's word according to its very nature and complete function. All of God's word is to be obeyed because it is authoritative, inerrant, and absolutely binding.

What is David's response to his own description of the written revelation of God? Look at verses 10-13.

Do you share the same response? What evidence is there in your own life that indicates that you see God's word as precious and obedience to it rewarding?

After reflecting on the words of creation and the words of the Lord, David reflects on his own words. Read Psalm 19 again, and then write out Psalm 19:14 as your own prayer based on the truths of this psalm.

This psalm was described by C.S. Lewis as "the greatest poem in the Psalter and one of the greatest lyrics in the world." [2] Theologians describe it as a psalm teaching that we can know something about God from His general revelation (creation) but that we can only correctly understand that general revelation through His specific revelation (the written word). We have seen that David was referring to the whole of Scripture in his comments.

What did Jesus say about the Scriptures in the following verses?

John 5:37-39

Luke 24:44-45

One of the most fascinating aspects of the arrangement of the Psalms is that each Torah psalm is followed immediately by a Messianic psalm or group of Messianic psalms. This presents the message that God's Word and God's Anointed are together the means for salvation and redemption.[3] This can even be seen in Psalm 19 – God's word is "more precious than gold" (v.10) because it points to the Redeemer (v.14b).

Prepare yourself for some information that may surprise you as we look once more at how the book of Psalms was arranged!

Psalm 1 – Torah Psalm
Psalm 2 – Messianic Psalm

Psalm 19 – Torah Psalm
Psalms 20 – 24 – Messianic Psalms

Psalm 119 – Torah Psalm
Psalms 120 – 134 – Messianic Psalms

What do you think about that?! I wonder if Jesus explained this to his disciples on the road to Emmaus. A Messianic Psalm not only prophesies the life and death of Christ, but also His reign as the Anointed King when He returns to the earth.

With this in mind, read once more the last phrase of Psalm 19, then read Psalm 20.

In what way does Psalm 20 connect to Psalm 19? Look for the meditations of the heart and the work of the Redeemer in Psalm 20.

That's quite enough to think on for this lesson. Just keep reading the Word of the Lord and trusting in His name. He will answer you when you call.

Arranging the Flowers

Psalm 20

"May He send you help from the sanctuary and support you from Zion!"
Psalm 20:2 [NAS]

This psalm opens with requests for help from the Lord. There is expectation, faith, hope, and confidence that the Lord will hear and that He will deliver. This is a call for the Anointed King to come from Zion as well as a prayer on His behalf and sets the stage for the next three psalms which will reflect the same messianic theme.

Psalm Twenty One

The last three psalms that we have studied were ones of personal prayer (Psalm 17), thanksgiving in victory (Psalm 18), and wisdom in God's revelation through nature and His word – one of the Torah psalms (Psalm 19). The psalm we will study today is, as you should expect based on what I shared at the end of the lesson on Psalm 19, a Messianic psalm. We will see that it clearly refers to the King who will return one day and defeat all His enemies.

Please read Psalm 21.

Respond with your reflections, questions, prayers or praise.

_____

_____

_____

_____

What specifically about the Lord is praised in the first and last verses?

As we learned during our study of Psalm 8, when the beginning and end are the same, this is called an "inclusio" and sets the stage for a key concept for the whole psalm.

What prophecy is given in Hannah's prayer in 1 Samuel 2:10?

Rather than trusting in his own strength, or in the strength of his horses and chariots (Psalm 20:7), the king trusts in the strength of the Lord. The king – the highest authority in Israel, the God-ordained ruler of the people, the most powerful official in the land – does not look to his own strength, but is shown in this psalm to depend on the strength of the Lord for his life, reputation, and his battles.

Take a deep look at your own perspective. What are your own strengths that you might depend on, rather than depending on the Lord?

The inclusio not only brings attention to the key theme of the strength of the Lord, but it also focuses our attention on the central verse of the psalm.

Which verse is at the center (the half-way point, the middle) of the psalm and what does it say?

Psalm 21 is actually the middle psalm in the Book One of the Psalms, and is important in its entirety because of its message. And verse 7 is the middle of Psalm 21, and is critical to our understanding of God's plan and His faithfulness. It is a definite reflection on the Davidic Covenant which was made between the Lord and King David.

Please note the promises of the covenant as found in 2 Samuel 7:12-16.

During your study of Psalm 17, you looked up the word "loving-kindness." The Hebrew word is "chesed" and it is used in 2 Samuel 7:15 as well as in Psalm 21:7. This word will continue to be used throughout the psalms and is known as a part of the covenant language. When used, it should bring to mind the promises that God made to David that he would have a descendent who would reign as king forever. Just as the words "life, liberty and the pursuit of happiness" bring the Declaration of Independence to the mind of Americans, so the words "chesed" and "anointed" and "king" would remind the Israelites of the Lord's covenant to David.

Even before the Lord made His promise to David, He spoke through the following prophecies indicating that there would be a majestic king ruling over all the earth one day. Note what is stated in these verses.

Genesis 49:10

Numbers 24:17

The background of the anticipation of a great King and the Davidic Covenant is so important for our study throughout the whole book of Psalms. We will repeatedly see the word "loving-kindness" and see that David trusts that the Lord will be faithful to His promises. This should be of great comfort to you, because the same Lord who will be faithful to His promises to David will be faithful to His promises to you.

The psalms give us the example of David, and the example of the Messiah, trusting the Lord in all circumstances of their life. David the king, and Messiah the King, are role models for us as we journey through the course of our lives. Keep this in mind as we study the through this book of Psalms. It will be especially meaningful to us when we come to Psalms 22 and 23.

Let's look at how the King is described in Psalm 21.

Please read Psalm 21:1-6 and list the specific blessings that the Lord bestows on the King.

Which of these blessings could not be applied to an earthly king, but only the Lord's Anointed King, His Son?

Two words are used in verse 5 to convey the stunning beauty and glory of the King – splendor and majesty. These words are found as a pair in several other Scriptures describing Yahweh. Look up the definitions of these words and then the cross-references.

Splendor: Strong's #1935
Hebrew word:
Hebrew definition:

Majesty: Strong's #1926
Hebrew word:
Hebrew definition:

1 Chronicles 16:25-27

Psalm 104:1-2

Psalm 111:2-3

There was a point in time when this splendid and majestic King allowed Himself to be seen in all His glory. How is Jesus described in the following passages?
Matthew 17:1-5

2 Peter 1:16-18

It overwhelms me to think that the great King, the Lord's Anointed, the Messiah is a man, yet He is God. The Old Testament passages do show us that no mere mortal man could fulfill the requirements and promises that the Lord made to the Israelites regarding their king. Only God Himself, in the person of Jesus, could do so. No one else can reign in righteousness, no one else can govern with true wisdom and sovreignty, no one else can provide true peace and prosperity. Let us bow down with reverence and adoration before our glorious King.

Read Psalm 21:8-12 and describe the future victory of the King. Look back at Psalm 2 to see the similarities in these two psalms.

According to 2 Thessalonians 1:6-10 –
Who will appear?

What will He do?

Why will He do it?

According to Revelation 19:11-16 –
Who will appear?

What will He do?

What is His name?

Psalm 21:7 is the central verse reflecting the Davidic Covenant and it also is a verse that explains why the King has been blessed and how the King will be able to defeat His enemies. Let's look at this verse again.

According to Psalm 21:7, why has the Lord given the King His heart's desire and such abundant blessings? And why will He be victorious over His enemies?

The phrase "trust in the Lord" is repeated 23 times throughout the psalms, and of course is a command found throughout all of Scripture. Look up the following verses and record a few which are meaningful to you.
Psalm 4:5

Psalm 31:6

Psalm 37:3, 5

Psalm 40:3

Psalm 73:28

Psalm 91:2

Psalm 118:8-9

Psalm 125:1

Even the great King, the coming Messiah, whom we know to be Jesus, is completely dependent on the Lord for all that He is and does. If Jesus is dependent and trusts the Lord, how much more so do we need to be? I know that "trusting the Lord" is easy to say but can be hard to do. I believe this is something that we learn to do, as we come to know the character of the Lord, and as we learn to let go of trusting in our own strength.

Please look up the following word:
Shaken: Strong's #4131
Hebrew word:
Hebrew definition:

Read Psalm 21:7 again, and rewrite it, personalizing it as a statement of your own dependence on the Lord.

Do you believe this? Do you live like you believe it? What are you experiencing right now that this truth will give you hope and confidence for as you endure it? Fill in the blank:

"In the midst of _____,

I trust in the Lord, and through the lovingkindness of My Most High God, I will not be shaken."

As we trust the Lord and see His faithfulness in our lives, we can say with David:

> " Be exalted, O Lord, in Your strength;
> We will sing and praise Your power."
> Psalm 21:13 ^{ESV}

Arranging the Flowers

Psalms 20, 21, and 22

While Psalm 21 is a grand psalm of the royal splendor of the Messiah and of victory over His enemies, and it is found in the middle of Book One as a centerpiece of hope, it is also has a very important place in relation to the psalms around it. First, it shows the answer to the prayer prayed in Psalm 20.

> Psalm 20:4 – May He grant you your heart's desire...
> ...   Psalm 21:2 –You have given him his heart's desire [NAS]

> Psalm 20:6, 9 – Now I know that the Lord saves His anointed...,
> ...   Psalm 21:1 – O Lord, in Your strength the king will be glad,
>   and in Your salvation how greatly he will rejoice! [NAS]

In addition, with Psalm 21:7 being the key verse of this psalm, the stage is set for an example of the King trusting the Lord in the deepest, darkest circumstances – that of His own death – as described in Psalm 22. Psalm 20 is a prayer for the Lord to answer and save the King, Psalm 21 is a statement of the strength of the Lord and the King's trust in Him, and Psalm 22 is a desperate cry for the Lord to answer and save (Psalm 22:19) as well as a declaration that the Lord has answered (Psalm 22:22-24). Psalm 22 truly testifies that through the loving-kindness of the Lord, the one who trusts in Him will not be shaken.

Psalm Twenty-Two

It is time now to approach a psalm with which you may be familiar as a prophecy of Christ's death on the cross. It begins with a deep lament, with an expression of devastating grief. But what we will find in this psalm may surprise you. It is a picture of one who is trusting in the Lord even during the most distressing time in his life, and it includes an exciting look at the promises of his future. While Psalm 21 was about the blessings and victory that the King receives because He trusts in the Lord, Psalm 22 describes the mysterious agony one can experience even when trusting in the Lord.

Please read Psalm 22.

Respond with your reflections, questions, prayers or praise.

_____

_____

_____

_____

This psalm has been described as the "Fifth Gospel" account of Christ's death on the cross. Under the inspiration of the Holy Spirit, David wrote the most detailed description of the crucifixion found anywhere in Scripture. While there is no question as to whether or not David wrote this, there is a difference of opinion regarding whether or not this relates to any specific experience of David's – or if it is solely a prophetic account of Christ's suffering.

There are a few observations that Dr. Steven Lawson makes that would indicate that this is prophecy alone:

First, there are no recorded events in the life of David that correspond to this event. Second, the psalm has specific phrases that could only be used of someone undergoing crucifixion. Third, unlike other psalms, this psalm contains no mention of the psalmist's personal sin, confession of sin, or even regret for the pains that he was suffering. Fourth, there is no call to God for vindication of wrongs suffered. [1]

What do you learn from 1 Peter 1:10-11?

With these observations and 1 Peter 1:11 in mind, we will study this psalm as a prophecy of Christ's suffering. Let us recognize at the same time that if we desire to "fellowship in the sufferings of Christ" (Phil. 3:10), then we too may experience times of great grief and trial. We can find an appropriate way to express our pain through the example given here.

Please record the phrases that express the agony that Christ was experiencing. Look at Psalm 22:1-18.

How does he describe God?

How does he describe himself?

How does he describe those around him?

Based on these observations, do you think that this cry for help came from a brief encounter with suffering or a prolonged one?

There are a series of contrasts described in these verses (1-18). Consider:

How did God respond to the Israelite fathers compared to how He responded to Christ?

How did God's response to Christ compare to how his enemies responded to him?

How did Christ's present experience compare to the time of his birth?

How often do you stop and think about the death of Christ and the agony He endured? It is a humbling, sobering, overwhelming thing to do. And we can't even really begin to grasp how horrible it was. What is described here is the worst hell any being will ever experience. Anyone else who experiences separation from God, or His wrath, or even His Fatherly discipline – deserves it. Jesus Christ did not deserve this suffering.

The following exercise is one which is more of contemplation than explanation. Please take time to meditate on what you read.

Please read Matthew 27:22-46. Observe that verses 35, 39, 43 and 46 are quotes or allusions to Psalm 22.

Read John 19:14-30. Psalm 22 is referenced in verses 23-24, and 28.

Please reflect on the agony Christ experienced as described in Psalm 22 and the passages you just read. Record your thoughts.

In the midst of His agony, according to Psalm 22:11, 19-21, Christ made several requests of God. What were they?

These are simple, uncomplicated pleas for help. Can you pray this way in the midst of your sufferings? Do you realize that no matter what trial you are going through, Christ can understand the pain of it? Because of His sufferings, He is our perfect Priest – meaning that He is the one who can understand our needs and present them to the Father on our behalf. (Hebrews 4:14-15)

Is there anything you need to simply cry out for help about right now? Looking at how Christ viewed the Lord, and how He asked for help, why don't you take time to pray according to His example?

Before we continue in studying the second half of this psalm, I'd like for you to think about the amount of time that Christ suffered. From the time of Judas' betraying kiss in the garden Thursday night - for almost the next 24 hours – Christ experienced agony. It was an eternity of suffering in a defined period of time.

Have you experienced a time of suffering – that seemed to go for an eternity? What is your perspective on how long you are willing to wait for God to answer your cries for help?

What expressions from Christ in this psalm do you think may help you endure a time of intense, unexplainable suffering?

We know Psalm 22 as one that describes the suffering of our Savior, but do you know that it also prophesies of His glorious kingdom to come? In the Hebrew, and certain translations, verse 21 ends on a note of triumph: "You have answered me!" and the whole mood of the psalm changes from then on.

Please read Psalm 22:22-31.

Verses 22-24 imply Christ's resurrection. To whom will He speak and what will He speak of? (To see verse 22 attributed to Christ, turn to Hebrews 2:10-12)

With verse 26 begins a description of the 1000 year reign of Christ – the Millennial Kingdom. What do believers have to look forward to? (There are other psalms which go into greater detail on this subject which we will study later.)

This psalm which began with such dark despair ends with a grand display of praise to the Lord because of His miraculous work on the cross. What does Psalm 22:30 - 31 declare?

It is fascinating that the last words of this psalm are equivalent in meaning to the last words of Jesus on the cross: "It is finished!" (John 19:30) Because the demands of our holy God were met by the sacrifice of Christ on the cross, all who believe in Jesus Christ will be made righteous by trusting in Him.

Let us therefore respond to Christ's words to us from this psalm:

> "You who fear the Lord – praise Him...
> and stand in awe of Him, all you descendants of Israel."
> Psalm 22:23 [NAS]

Psalm Twenty-Three

We have come to one of the most cherished of all blooms in the arrangement of our bouquet. Like a deep red rose, this psalm is elegant, but simple; richly scented with scenes from the meadows; marked with thorns of danger; and it carries the message of the love of the Lord. Receive it today as a gift, and take time to appreciate all that it has to communicate to you.

Please read Psalm 23.

Respond with your reflections, questions, prayers or praise.

_____

_____

_____

_____

This is the type of Scripture that almost seems too beautiful, too meaningful in its entirety to examine in an in-depth manner. If you did not enjoy a quiet moment with the Lord during your reading of it, please go back and just take time to be still and quiet as you read it once again.

I'd like for you to see a literal translation of this psalm from the Hebrew:

¹ Yahweh is the one who shepherds me
  I will not lack
² In pastures of grass He will cause me to lie down
  By waters of refreshment He will lead me
³ My soul He will restore
  He will guide me in paths of righteousness for the sake of His name
⁴ Even when I walk in the valley of the deepest shadow
  I will not fear evil because You are with me
  Your rod and Your staff - they comfort me
⁵ You will arrange before me a table in sight of those who show hostility
  You have anointed with oil my head, my cup is saturated
⁶ Surely! Goodness and lovingkindness (chesed) will pursue me all the days of my life
  And I will return to the house of Yahweh for days without end.

What is the very first word of this psalm? Is this word repeated at any time?

What does this tell you? Remember "inclusio" – this sets the theme for the whole psalm. Who is being referred to as the Shepherd?

As believers who spend much time in the New Testament and cherish the words of Christ, we are very familiar with His statement that He is the Good Shepherd, and that He is the Shepherd who lays down His life for His sheep. But before Jesus made that statement, God the Father declared and proved that He was the Shepherd of Israel. Look at the following references that show how God showed Himself as the Shepherd.

What do you learn about who the Shepherd is and what He does from the following verses?
Genesis 48:14-15

Genesis 49:22-25

Deuteronomy 2:7

Psalm 78:52-53

Psalm 80:1

Psalm 100:3

Isaiah 40:11

What we don't realize is how shocking it must have been for the Israelites who looked to God as their Shepherd, and probably loved Psalm 23 as much as we do, to hear Jesus say that He is the Good Shepherd!

I know you are probably so familiar with this psalm that the following questions in this lesson may seem too simple, but the truths that they will highlight make a tremendous difference in our lives.

According to verse 2, what actions does Yahweh carry out?

Please look up the definitions for the following words:
Pastures: Strong's #4999
Hebrew word:
Hebrew definition:

Quiet: Strong's #4496
Hebrew word:
Hebrew definition:

Only when sheep sense that they are safe will they lie down to rest, and only when rushing waters are dammed up into a quiet pool will they drink. Sheep are fearful animals – what about you?

Do you find security and peace in the Lord's provision for you? If yes, then does your life show it?

Look at verse 3. What two things does Yahweh do for us and why?

The following verses indicate the same idea. Read them and note – what does Yahweh do for us and why? Understanding *why* is as critical as understanding *what*.
1 Samuel 12:22

Psalm 106:8

Isaiah 43:25

Ezekiel 36:21-27

Because we already observed that this psalm uses the poetic device of inclusio, we can expect that the central verse of the psalm is of great importance. Verse 4 is the longest verse, and expresses the most extreme circumstance.

Read Psalm 23:4 and note the experience according to the categories below:

Place of crisis:

Perspective during crisis:

Reason for perspective:

Comfort during crisis:

"The shadow of death" is a compound noun in the Hebrew, with the literal sense of a "very deep shadow" or even "total darkness." The Israelites wandered through the "deep shadow" of the wilderness (Jer. 2:6), and Job used this word to express the threat of death which he experienced (Job 10:21-22). This Hebrew word is used to convey a most extreme situation and danger. Whether your crisis is one of grief over the death of a loved one, loss of a job, infertility, divorce, financial concerns, health issues, consequences of sin, or any other life experience that makes you feel like you are going to die or you want to die.... if you know that the Lord is your shepherd, you do not need to fear – because He is with you. The Lord declares this repeatedly.

Please note the truths from the following verses:
Genesis 15:1

Deuteronomy 31:6

Psalm 139:7-12

Isaiah 41:10

I'd like to affirm to you that the previous verses from the Old Testament, while spoken to specific individuals or to the Israelite community, are appropriate promises for us to believe because Jesus Himself as well as other New Testament authors communicated the same truths.

Please record what you learn from the following comforting verses:
Matthew 28:18-20

John 14:16-18

Romans 8:35-39

Hebrews 13:5-6

Being comforted, we can now experience other things that God has in store for us. While some see the analogy of the shepherd continuing into verses 5 and 6, it is also probable that the description of the Lord changes to that of being a host – one who invites a guest to a banquet.

Read Psalm 23:5-6. How are the actions of the host similar to the actions of the shepherd?

The last verse of this psalm is as rich and beautiful as the first. Please write out Psalm 23:6.

I'm going to ask you to look up two words – please indulge me!!
Goodness: Strong's #2896
Hebrew word:
Hebrew definition:

Mercy: Strong's #2617
Hebrew word:
Hebrew definition:

Surprise! There's that extra-special, covenant word again – chesed! I'm going to repeat what I shared with you when we first encountered this word:

> From the book of Psalms, we learn that divine chesed saves people from disaster or oppressors. We are constantly surrounded by the threats of natural disasters, hostile enemies, and our own fleshly weaknesses. We turn to God to plead for him to save us according to His chesed and we realize that God's faithful, loyal love is the only thing that protects us from disaster. We must, however, discover His loving-kindness, His faithfulness, at each new crisis. And while we can be assured that He will see us through the trials, the pain of the trial is rarely fully removed.

That's a very appropriate commentary on this word in light of the danger encountered in this psalm.

Please read once again all of Psalm 23, in the literal Hebrew translation that I gave you earlier. What does verse 6 say literally?

More than one commentator sees this verse as meaning "I shall return and dwell in the house of the Lord." This is important to observe, especially when we look at the context of this psalm. Psalm 20 and 21 were about the anointed King – the Messiah, Psalm 22 was about the suffering of the Messiah, and Psalm 24 which we will study in our next lesson is about the return and entrance of the King (the Messiah) into the temple of the Lord. Please consider that the previous 3 psalms and the following psalm are messianic. Psalm 23 has messianic overtones as well.

While David was an anointed king and experienced the shepherding of the Lord, and while we are also considered to be sheep, so too was the Messiah – the Lamb of the Lord. Psalm 22 presents the time that the Lamb was sacrificed, and Psalm 23 shows how the Lamb trusted in His Shepherd when He walked through the valley of the shadow of death. Because of His lovingkindness, because of His faithfulness to His covenant, for His own Name's sake, Yahweh was the Shepherd to His Servant Jesus and delivered Him through His darkest hours – and will lead Him back to the house of the Lord to dwell there and reign for eternity.

Does this perspective of Psalm 23 take away its personal application to you? Not at all. Jesus is the one we are to follow – if He trusted the Lord as His Shepherd, then so too should we.

Walking with the Shepherd

The Lord is my Shepherd,
> *I am His lamb,*
I shall not want,
> *All I need is in His hands.*
He maketh me lie down in green pastures,
> *I rest in His tender embrace.*
He leadeth me beside the still waters,
> *I look up and see His face.*
He restoreth my soul, and leadeth me,
> *His outstretched hand I take,*
Down paths of righteousness we walk,
> *For His name's sake.*
Yea, though I walk through the valley,
> *That is dark and dismal and bleak,*
Even in the shadow of death,
> *I know I am one He will keep.*
I will fear no evil,
> *For He is always with me,*
His rod and His staff give me comfort,
> *With instruction and love He leads.*

He prepareth a table before me,
The bread of life feeds my soul,
In the presence of my enemies,
He gives me blessings more precious than gold.
He anointeth my head with oil,
He clothes me in garments of praise,
My cup runneth over and over,
I will worship Him all of my days.
Surely, goodness and mercy will follow me,
Peace and joy will walk with me too,
For all of the days of my life,
Every morning His kindness is new.
And forever I will dwell,
Of this I am assured,
In the place He has prepared for me,
The beautiful house of the Lord.

Psalm Twenty-Four

If this psalm were a flower, I think it would be a grand lily to trumpet, to herald the coming of our King! After anticipation (Psalm 20), expectation (Psalm 21), affliction (Psalm 22), and assurance (Psalm 23), it is time for exaltation. Psalm 24 exalts the King of Glory as He enters the city.

Please read Psalm 24.

Respond with your reflections, questions, prayers or praise.

_____

_____

_____

_____

During my first reading of this psalm in studying today, the first two verses seemed strange to me – disconnected. I wondered what they had to do with the psalm as a whole.

What does Psalm 24:1-2 tell you? If you read verse 1, and then ask "why?", you'll find the answer in verse 2.

In verse 2, we observed the statement that the Lord established the earth upon the seas. This same Hebrew word is used again in Scripture to refer to the establishment of the Davidic dynasty.

Even though we have already looked at this passage a few times in our previous studies, please turn again to 2 Samuel 7:12-16. What does the Lord promised to "establish"?

The language used in these two verses takes us back to Genesis 1, when God created the heavens and the earth. Then, there seems to be an abrupt shift in thought between verses 2 and 3. As I pondered this, it occurred to me that if I were thinking about the sovereign God who created the earth, I would also reflect on His awesome nature. And who could approach such a great one, such a holy one? That question is asked, which we also saw asked in Psalm 15. The answer which is given is similar, but expanded from that given in the earlier psalm.

According to Psalm 24:3-4, who may go up into the holy mountain of God? How does this reflect the inner character and outer behavior of someone?

Look at verse 5. What will this one who approaches the Lord receive?

Do you think this means that a person's behavior would be the basis of his entering the presence of the Lord?

It is important to remember that only one with a pure heart can approach the Lord. The Lord looks on the heart and knows whether one approaches Him by faith or not. The Old Testament saints' relationships and righteousness were always based on faith. The "Hall of Faith" in Hebrews 11 shows us this, along with many other passages.

How does Psalm 24:6 continue with this thought?

Please look up the following words from this verse:

"those who *seek* Him"
Seek: Strong's #1875
Hebrew word:
Hebrew definition:

"who *seek* Your face"
Seek: Strong's #1245
Hebrew word:
Hebrew definition:

The greatest promise, and blessing, is that those who seek the Lord will find Him. Here He comes!

Read Psalm 24:7-10.
Look at the repeated phrases from the passage you just read.

What action is to be taken?

By whom?

Why?

The gates were the place of the administration of an ancient city. Elders and officials and tradesmen would conduct their affairs there. The "gates" and "doors" symbolize the people of the city.

What were the people commanded to do?

Who is the King of glory and how is He described?

Please look up the following word:

Host: Strong's #6635   **(see also "Lord of Hosts" in Bible dictionaries)**
Hebrew word:
Hebrew definition:

He is strong and mighty in all battles, but let's look at the one most recently mentioned in Psalms.

Read Psalm 21:8-13.

Who is the King of glory? Who is the King in Psalm 21? What did we discover about the King in Psalm 21 – is he just a man? How do Psalm 24: 8 and 10 repeat the description of the King given in Psalm 21?

Do you find it challenging to grasp the descriptions of the King as a man who is also clearly referred to as God? Do you find it just a little bit difficult to understand the reality of the Trinity? I certainly do! We will see this over and over again, as we have already seen in several psalms. Yahweh is the Most High God, and His Son is His Anointed King who is God.

According to Deuteronomy 33:1-5, who was the King over Israel?

According to 1 Samuel 10:17-19, what did the Israelites do?

This was not a good idea! The books of 1 and 2 Kings show that Israel and Judah were taken from the land of Israel into captivity because neither the kings nor the people followed the commands given by the Lord through Moses. Four main themes in the book of Deuteronomy serve as the standard against which all the kings described in the book of Kings were tested:

1) *the king and the people were to show absolute allegiance to the one true God;*
2) *the king and the people were to worship the Lord in the specific manner prescribed by Him;*
3) *the king was to serve as the spiritual leader for the people of the nation;*
4) *the king and the people were to heed the words spoken by men of God — the prophets.*

The book of Kings records from a theological perspective the practices of the kings of both the Northern Kingdom and the Southern Kingdom, showing that a pattern of failure began during the reign of Solomon and continued to the point that the Lord judged the nation by sending them into exile. But the Lord gave hope through His prophets for a glorious kingdom to be established.

According to Isaiah 9:6-7, who is the King who will reign on the throne of David? Is He man or God?

We are pondering the deep mysteries of the Godhead right now. I'd like you to see one more description of the King of Glory. Many commentators look at Psalm 24 as a song used to celebrate the entrance of the ark of the covenant into the temple, with the ark being the very representation of Yahweh. This is probably historical reality, but there is a future reality that should be recognized when reading this psalm as well. The last chapters of the book of Ezekiel describe the Millennial reign of Christ over the earth. Following His defeat of the kings of the earth (Ps. 2:9; Ps. 21:8-12; Rev. 19:11-21), He will take His place on the throne.

According to Ezekiel 43:1-7, who ascends the throne, how is He described, and what does He say about His reign?

Please read Psalm 24 again.

The Lord reigns as King over His creation, and only those whose lives reflect righteousness may enter His presence. What has impacted you the most about this psalm?

Sometimes we need to be told to look up and see the King of Glory. I hope this psalm has prompted you to behold Him in His glory today.

Arranging the Flowers:

On more than one occasion, the Scriptures describe the Millennial Kingdom as one in which people will desire to go to the temple of the Lord, and to seek the ways of the Lord: His wisdom, instruction, and guidance (Zec. 8:20-23; Isa. 2:2-3). Psalms 25 — 30 are a cluster of psalms that draw attention to these two themes.

Psalm 25

> "The secret of the Lord is for those who fear Him,
> and He will make them know His covenant."
> Psalm 25:14 NAS

Psalm 24 speaks of the generation of those who seek the face of the Lord, and Psalm 25 picks up this theme. It is an acrostic psalm which typically indicates that the author is focusing on one specific theme; here it is that of seeking the Lord's instruction. "Make me know Your ways, O Lord; teach me Your paths. Lead me in Your truth and teach me, for You are the God for my salvation; for You I wait all the day." (Psalm 25:4-5) Not only does this psalm show the heart of one who is seeking the Lord, but it also shows that the one seeking the Lord knows that he must have clean hands and a pure heart (Psalm 24:4) to enter the presence of the Lord and therefore he asks for forgiveness of his sins: "For Your name's sake, O Lord, pardon my iniquity, for it is great" (Psalm 25:11).

Psalm 26

The mention of the house of the Lord (His dwelling place, the temple) in Psalm 23:6 introduced the desire for and delight in being in the Lord's presence, and it was further highlighted in Psalm 24:3. In Psalm 26, we see David repeatedly declaring his determination and desire to be with the Lord. He blends the instructions from Psalm 1, 15, and 24 together with the prayers from Psalm 25 to show that he is following the ways of the Lord and wants to be among those who praise the Lord at the temple. The italicized phrases correspond to the previous psalms noted in parentheses.

1. Vindicate me, O LORD, *for I have walked in my integrity,* (Psalm 15:2)
   And *I have trusted* in the LORD without wavering. (Psalm 25:2)
2. Examine me, O LORD, and try me;
   Test my mind and my heart.
3. For *Your lovingkindness* is before my eyes, (Psalm 25:6)
   And I have walked in *Your truth.* (Psalm 25:6, 10)
4. *I do not sit with deceitful men,*
   Nor will I go with pretenders.
5. *I hate the assembly of evildoers,*
   And I will not sit with the wicked. (Psalm 1:1)
6. *I shall wash my hands in innocence,* (Psalm 24:4)
   And I will go about *Your altar,* O LORD, (Psalm 24:3)
7. That I may proclaim with the voice of thanksgiving
   And declare all Your wonders.
8. O LORD, I love the *habitation of Your house* (Psalm 24:3)
   And the *place where Your glory dwells.* (Psalm 24:3)
9. Do not take my soul away along with sinners,
   Nor my life with men of bloodshed,
10. In whose hands is a wicked scheme,
    And whose right hand is full of bribes.
11. But as for me, *I shall walk in my integrity;* (Psalm 15:2; Psalm 25:21)
    Redeem me, and be gracious to me. (Psalm 25:16, 21)
12. My foot stands on a level place;
    In the *congregations* I shall bless the LORD. ᴺᴬˢ

Psalm 26 stresses the importance of single-hearted devotion to the Lord and a life that evidences that devotion. True worship of the Lord will be expressed through a life of integrity. The Lord's great love – His unfailing lovingkindness – His sacrificial love – should overwhelm us and motivate us to wholehearted worship of the Lord in every aspect of our lives.

Psalm Twenty-Seven

*After seeing an expression of single-hearted devotion in Psalm 26, it is appropriate to see a declaration and prayer of that devotion in Psalm 27. This psalm is a favorite of mine, and I have found comfort, peace, and my life's pursuit in it. My "life-verse" is Psalm 27:4, which summarizes the passion of my life that is the foundation of everything that I do and say. In the ministry, in the mundane, in the moment by moment of each day – the **one thing** that I ask of the Lord is to dwell in His house and to behold His beauty. We'll learn what that means in our lesson today, and encourage ourselves in the Lord even as David did as he wrote this psalm.*

Please read Psalm 27.

Respond with your reflections, questions, prayers or praise.

_____

_____

_____

_____

What is the most meaningful part of this psalm to you?

David begins with a declaration of confidence in Yahweh. How does he describe the Lord in Psalm 27:1?

The first words of this psalm, in English and in Hebrew, are short, to the point, and actually easy to miss. "The Lord is my light." Let's spend some time making sure we understand what that means.

The metaphor, light, implies a force that automatically dispels darkness (here representing the psalmist's enemies); the language is reminiscent of Psalm 23:4, in which fearlessness is expressed despite death's dark shadow. But the metaphor may also be associated specifically with military dangers, as is implied by the same kind of language in Psalm 18:29. Thus the psalmist is affirming that even in the darkness of the terrible threat of war, he has no fear, for God is the light that can dispel such darkness. [1]

Let's look at a few other verses that show the Lord giving light. Record what you learn.
Exodus 10:21-23

Exodus 13:21

The Lord gives His light to us in a different way than He did for the Israelites. According to the following verses, how can you "turn on" the light of the Lord?
Psalm 43:3

Psalm 119:105

John 8:12

2 Peter 1:19

It is easy to say "The Lord is my light…", but I hope that when you pray and say these words, they will really mean something to you. Based on our study so far, would you put into your own words your understanding of the how the Lord is your light and how His light relieves your fears?

The first verse is just the beginning to David's declaration of confidence and trust in the Lord. He affirms that whether wicked men, enemies, or even an army might attack him, he will trust in God's protection of him. He closes the description of dark and fearful times with a strong assertion of his perspective. The NAS translates it this way:

"Though war rise against me, in spite of this, I will be confident."
Psalm 27:3 NAS

The next verse is the key to his confidence. What does Psalm 27:4 tell you about David?

Let's highlight the "who, what, when, where, why, and how" in this verse.
Who is David's focus on?

What actions does David say that he has taken or will take? (What are the verbs?)

Where does he want to be?

When does he want to be there?

Why does he want to be there?

How is he going to achieve this goal?

It's interesting to note that this is the only occurrence of this type of phrase in Scripture. It is one of the most single-minded statements of purpose to be found anywhere in the Old Testament. [2]

Please look up the definitions for the following words:
Seek: Strong's #1245
(turn back to pg. 56, the same word is used in Psalm 24)
Hebrew word:
Hebrew definition:

Dwell: Strong's #3427
Hebrew word:
Hebrew definition:

Temple: Strong's #1964
Hebrew word:
Hebrew definition:

> Let us especially note that our word [temple] does not occur in the OT until 1 Samuel… after the kingship was established in Israel. This meaning (God's palace) occurs in the psalmists' prayers when they describe the life of blessedness. Figuratively, David prays that he, too, may dwell in God's house/temple (Psalm 27:4). He surely does not ask for a change in God's law whereby he, a non-priest, could enter (indeed, dwell in) the temple. So it is a state of blessedness for which he prays, that he might always be in God's favor. No doubt, it is God's earthly palace/temple toward which David directs his prayer, although it is God Himself whom he addresses. God is not limited spatially to the temple. However, God's chosen place is His temple and it is to be respected in proportion to the respect due to the Creator. [3]

What do you learn about the temple of the Lord from Solomon's prayer in 1 Kings 8:27-30?

What attitude about the house of the Lord is found in Psalm 84?

The one thing that David desired was to be in the presence of the Lord... "to behold the beauty of the Lord and to inquire in His temple".

Please look up the following words:
Beauty: Strong's #5278
Hebrew word:
Hebrew definition:

Inquire: Strong's #1239
Hebrew word:
Hebrew definition:

Do you seek to behold the beauty of the Lord? Do you believe that the Lord is delightful? Do you spend time contemplating His being and nature, and your own nature in contrast to His?

To earnestly pursue the Lord, to remain in His presence, to admire the delightfulness of His being, and to contemplate on Him and His ways... this was David's heartbeat.

How did the Lord describe David in Acts 13:22?

And now, it's time to make it personal. Consider your daily routine. Think about how you spend your time, your money, and your energy. Why do you do what you each day? What is the motivating goal of your life?

Perhaps you have asked the Lord to bring you into His presence and to allow you to experience His beauty, grace, and wisdom. But have you also sought that yourself, as David said that he did.... "One thing I ask of the Lord, *this I will seek....*" ? (NIV) Have you added effort and discipline to your desire? How?

Because of David's relationship with the Lord, his pursuit of His presence, and his confidence in His protection, he cries out in time of need. The rest of this psalm shows David's trust in the Lord and specific requests from Him.

According to Psalm 27:5-6, what does David believe that God will do for him, and what is his response to that?

According to Psalm 27:7-12, what are David's specific requests?

David had one trial after another, enduring the threats of enemies and encountering wars. One account shows that David practiced what he prayed.

Please read 1 Samuel 23:1-14. What is the setting, how did David handle the situation, and how did the Lord respond?

Just as David began Psalm 27 with confidence in the Lord to protect and deliver him, he ends with confidence as well. What does he believe according to Psalm 27:13?

What do you believe with the same faith and confidence?

Finally, this psalm ends with a strong exhortation to its audience. It is one that we need to heed on a daily basis. The Hebrew uses strong, imperative verb forms. Please write out the four phrases from Psalm 27:14 with capital letters and exclamation points!

- _____

- _____

- _____

- _____

David had more than one occasion to wait on the Lord. This verse from 1 Samuel 30:6 summarizes quite a terrible time, and how David handled it.

"Now David was greatly distressed, for the people spoke of stoning him, because the soul of all the people was grieved, every man for his sons and his daughters. But David strengthened himself in the LORD his God." [NKJ]

Do you know how to strengthen yourself in the Lord? The exhortation from Psalm 27:14 is a great truth to preach to yourself! In all capitals and with exclamation points!

Please look up the following word:

Wait: Strong's #6960
Hebrew word:
Hebrew definition:

This word is used for the first time in the psalms in Psalm 25:3, 5 and 21. What do you learn from these verses?

This same word is also used in Isaiah 40:31. What can you expect when you wait on the Lord?

This word was also used by Jeremiah in his darkest days and greatest grief, after the destruction of Jerusalem and the Lord's temple. Even so, he was able to trust in the Lord and say:

> The LORD is good to those who wait for Him,
> To the person who seeks Him. Lamentations 3:25 [NAS]

Please read Psalm 27 in its entirety again. What two, or three, or maybe four words would you choose to summarize the heart of this psalm?

Psalm 27 is a reflection of the life of one who is living out the instructions and promises of Psalm 1 and 2. There are several words used in this psalm that were used in those first two psalms.

Please read Psalm 1:1-2 and the last phrase of Psalm 2:12. How is Psalm 27 the testimony of one following the counsel of these psalms?

One thing.... What is your one thing? I hope today's lesson has helped you think about what your life is all about.

Give me one pure and holy passion
Give me one magnificent obsession
Give me one glorious ambition for my life
To know and follow hard after you

To know and follow hard after you
To grow as your disciple in your truth
This world is empty, pale, and poor
Compared to knowing you my Lord
Lead me on and I will run after you
Lead me on and I will run after you[4]

Arranging the Flowers

Psalm 28

A Psalm of David.
To Thee, O LORD, I call; My rock, do not be deaf to me,
lest, if Thou be silent to me, I become like those who go down to the pit.
²Hear the voice of my supplications when I cry to Thee for help,
when I lift up my hands toward Thy holy sanctuary. NAS
Psalm 28:1 NAS

Psalm 28 continues with the theme of God's presence in the temple, and the psalmist's desire to be in His presence. But in this psalm, David appears to have not felt the presence of the Lord for some time. He calls out with desperate urgency and pleas for the Lord to hear and answer him. He doesn't want to be treated as the wicked will be – separated from the Lord. Then there is a sudden change in the outlook of this prayer, apparently David *did* hear from the Lord; so he praises Him as his strength and his shield.

Isn't this just like what we experience all the time? Circumstances and our own thoughts can make us doubt the Lord's presence, and then we desperately cry out… "Speak to me!" And He does, and we are reassured.

Blessed be the LORD, Because He has heard the voice of my supplication.
The LORD is my strength and my shield; My heart trusts in Him, and I am helped;
Therefore my heart exults, And with my song I shall thank Him.
Psalm 28:6-7 NAS

Psalm Twenty-Nine

Wow. That's what Psalm 29 makes me say! In the past several psalms, the focus has been on the Lord's presence in His house – the temple. And in Psalm 27 and 28, there is a very clear desire on David's part to behold the Lord (Ps. 27:4) , and to hear from Him (Ps. 28:1-2). Now we come to Psalm 29 which describes the Lord showing up, making some noise, and displaying His strength.

Please read Psalm 29.

Respond with your reflections, questions, prayers or praise.

_____

_____

_____

_____

Let's begin at the heading of this psalm. What does it say?

It's a little surprising that we haven't looked up the word *psalm* yet. This is a good time to do it.

Psalm: Strong's #4210

Hebrew word:

Hebrew definition:

While we have been calling each chapter in this book a "psalm", actually, not every one of them is entitled that way. The previous two chapters (27 and 28) had as their title in Hebrew "of David". My Bible has italicized the word psalm in their headings. What I want you to realize is that Psalm 29 is actually a song.

Now that we have that settled, let's look back at another connection between Psalm 27, 28, and 29. What does David say he will do in the following verses?

Psalm 27:6

Psalm 28:7

Psalm 29 follows Psalms 27 and 28 as a song of exaltation and thanks. It has a lot of repetition, rhyming and word play in the Hebrew. I would love to have heard it sung by the Levitical choir!

Please underline the repeated phrases, and highlight each occurrence of "the LORD". (Remember, all capital letters means that this is Yahweh.)

¹ Ascribe to the LORD, O sons of the mighty,

   Ascribe to the LORD glory and strength.

² Ascribe to the LORD the glory due to His name;

   Worship the LORD in holy array.

³ The voice of the LORD is upon the waters;

The God of glory thunders,

The LORD is over many waters.

4   The voice of the LORD is powerful,

The voice of the LORD is majestic.

5   The voice of the LORD breaks the cedars;

Yes, the LORD breaks in pieces the cedars of Lebanon.

6   He makes Lebanon skip like a calf,

And Sirion like a young wild ox.

7   The voice of the LORD hews out flames of fire.

8   The voice of the LORD shakes the wilderness;

The LORD shakes the wilderness of Kadesh.

9   The voice of the LORD makes the deer to calve

And strips the forests bare;

And in His temple everything says, "Glory!"

10   The LORD sat as King at the flood;

Yes, the LORD sits as King forever.

11   The LORD will give strength to His people;

The LORD will bless His people with peace. ^{NAS}

This song begins with a call to worship. What are the listeners instructed to do in verses 1 and 2?

The majority of the song describes the sounds and impacts of a severe thunderstorm which David viewed as an expression of the supremacy of God. The word "voice" which is repeated over and over, is an ordinary Hebrew word which can mean voice or sound. This psalm may be easier for you to grasp if you read it replacing "voice" with "sound".

This psalm describes the impact of the "voice of the Lord". What actions are described in verses 3 - 9? (Look for the active verbs.)

The skipping of Lebanon and Sirion refers to "their being shaken by the crash of the thunder-a feature in the picture which certainly does not rest upon what is actually true in nature, but figuratively describes the apparent quaking of the earth during a heavy thunderstorm." [1]

I would like for you to think about your own experiences during a strong thunderstorm. What do you see, hear, and feel? Do you think this psalm captures that type of experience?

Now let's look at a few storms recorded in Scripture.

What happened in 1 Samuel 7:10?

What happened in Exodus 9:22-28?

What happened and why, according to Genesis 6:5-7, 7:11-12, 21-22?

The key to understanding Psalm 29 is in verse 10. What truth is declared here?

A king is a sovereign ruler, one with all power and authority. How is this shown in this psalm?

While the pagan communities surrounding the Israelites would have attributed the forces of nature to the whims of their gods, the Israelites recognized that the Lord is the King over nature. Today, many around the world might call a natural disaster an "act of God", but they more often attribute authority to "Mother Nature."

It amuses me that weather is a safe topic for casual conversation... you know – just stay away from those controversial topics like politics and faith. But – Psalm 29 plus many other Scriptures teach us that the weather is under God's control!

What do you learn about God's sovereignty over nature from Job 37:2-13?

Remember that we began by recognizing that Psalm 29 is a song, which appropriately followed Psalms 27 and 28. David had made requests of the Lord, and had called out to Him to repay his enemies for the evil practices. We've just realized that the Lord shows His judgment against His enemies through storms, and for this, David worships the Lord. But during the storm, the Lord also is a refuge for His people.

What does Psalm 29:11 tell you about our great God, who thunders out judgment against the wicked?

Now that we have the whole psalm in mind and hopefully understand it a little better, let's look at it again and concentrate on one other repeated concept.

Please read Psalm 29 again.

Fill in the following blanks:

¹ Ascribe to the LORD, O sons of the mighty,

   Ascribe to the LORD_____ and strength.

² Ascribe to the LORD the _____ due to _____;

   Worship the LORD in holy array.

³ The voice of the LORD is upon the waters;

   The God of _____ thunders...

⁹ And in His temple everything says, "_____!"

Please look up the meaning for:
Glory: Strong's #3519
Hebrew word:
Hebrew definition:

What do you see about God in Psalm 29 that prompts you to honor Him?

What do you see about God in the following Scriptures that prompts you to honor Him?
Psalm 108:4-5

Psalm 113:4-9

Psalm 138:2-7

We shouldn't complete our contemplation of the glory of God without hearing from the voice of the Lord Himself, when He described Himself and caused His glory to pass by Moses.

What do you learn about God in Exodus 33:18, 34:5-7?

How did Moses respond to the seeing and hearing the God of glory (Exodus 34:8)?

In Exodus, the Lord hid Moses in a rock when His glory passed by. In Psalm 29, the Lord blessed His people with strength and peace during the midst of the storm, when His glory passed by. What we can learn from these experiences is that knowing our God of glory is the safest refuge from any storm or circumstance. He is sovereign over all weather, all events, and all the earth. Our greatest protection and peace will come when we ascribe to Him the glory due to His name.

The glory of the Lord is the sum total of all of His divine perfections and attributes. It is the essence of who God is – it is infinite, immeasurable, and inexhaustible. Please take time now to write a song, a poem, or a prayer to the Lord, honoring Him with the praise that His glorious name deserves.

Sing the glory of His name;
Make His praise glorious.
Psalm 66:2 ^{NAS}

Arranging the Flowers

Psalm 30

Once again, I find myself having great difficulty in choosing which psalms we should study! Psalm 30 has in it's title "a Song at the Dedication of the House – a Psalm of David". It so appropriately follows Psalm 29 which led everyone in the temple to shout "Glory!" to the Lord. While the title of Psalm 30 tells us when it was used, the content of the psalm tells us of David's thankfulness for God's deliverance through a time of crisis. This psalm is a reminder to us that our hope is in the Lord. "Weeping may endure for a night, but joy comes in the morning." (Psalm30:5 ^{NKV}) The times of joy will come, we just have to wait for them.

Psalm Thirty-One

Let me prepare you for our study today by telling you that this is a long psalm. I almost chose not to do a lesson on it, but, Jesus quotes from this psalm, and I didn't want to miss sharing that with you. It's similar to Psalm 22 in that it is an expression of trust in the Lord and cry for His help during a time of great suffering. For those of you who may be experiencing a time of difficulty and desperation, I hope that this psalm will help you trust the Lord.

Please read Psalm 31.

Respond with your reflections, questions, prayers or praise.

_____

_____

_____

_____

This psalm is similar to Psalm 30 in that we see David praying to the Lord for His help during a time of trouble. David is an example of one who trusts in the Lord's faithfulness.

How does David describe his trials according to the following verses?
Verse 4

Verses 8-13

What are David's specific prayer requests in the following verses?
Verse 1

Verse 2

Verse 9

Verses 15-17

I could suggest at this point that you take David's requests and make them your own, but following a formula for prayer is worthless if your words are not expressions of your own faith.

Woven throughout this psalm are David's declarations of his knowledge of the Lord's character and His personal relationship with him. David's awareness of his trial and his prayer requests are founded on the truth of who God is and who He is to David. Let's strengthen our faith as we look at the faithfulness of the Lord.

In the following verses, record the statements that David makes about the Lord, as he addresses Him "In You…", "My….", or "You ….. (are, have, will, etc.)".

Verses 1-5

Verses 7-8

Verses 14-15

Verse 19-21

We've seen the trouble described, and we've seen David's specific prayer requests. In the midst of the trial, David expresses his faith in the Lord. Do you find that you are able to do the same? It can be very difficult to remember and believe in the goodness and faithfulness of the Lord when you are right in the middle of pain and suffering. It is so important to be able to declare the truth of who the Lord is even when you don't feel like you are experiencing His goodness and love.

Please take this opportunity to declare the truth of who the Lord is in your own words. Base your statement on David's declarations that you recorded above. You can make this a prayer or statement to be shared with others.

Do you believe this?

Please turn to and read Hebrews 11:1-6. What is so important about faith?

Immediately following the chapter affirming the biblical heroes of faith, the author of Hebrews gives us an exhortation.

What does Hebrews 12:1-3 tell us to do?

What does Hebrews 12:1-3 tell us about Jesus?

We recently looked at Psalm 22 and the suffering of Christ on the cross. As I mentioned earlier, Jesus quotes Psalm 31:5. Let's look at Luke's version of the crucifixion where this verse is recorded.

Please read Luke 23:33-46.

What type of suffering do you see Christ experiencing that is similar to the trials described in Psalm 31?

Psalm 31:9 -13 describe the physical suffering that the psalmist experienced, and we know enough about the terrible death through crucifixion to know that this type of physical suffering was experienced by Christ on the cross as well. One commentary's note on Psalm 31:9 is: "The psalmist seems to be lamenting that his breathing is impaired because of the physical and emotional suffering he is forced to endure." [1] *It's a very scary thing when you feel like you can't breathe. Those of you who suffer from asthma or anxiety attacks can certainly relate to this.*

I'd like to encourage each of you to read this psalm again, and choose a verse or phrase that you can commit to memory and call to mind during times of trouble.

Write out the verse you chose.

In verse 22, David says something that I think is very interesting and that we need to consider. Read this verse and explain what he meant.

The NET Bible translates it this way: "I jumped to conclusions and said, 'I am cut off from your presence!' But you heard my plea for mercy when I cried out to you for help."

Do you ever do that?! Jump to conclusions? And come to the wrong conclusion about the Lord? Do you have any comments that you regularly make that are not true about the Lord? Do you say things like: "The Lord doesn't love me", "God's angry with me", or "God's not answering my prayers"? Maybe you don't say it, but you think it. Do you doubt His goodness and love?

Please read and write out Psalm 31:14.

If you can say "You are my God" with David, then you can be assured that the Lord loves you, His "anger" is the loving discipline of a father, and He hears your prayers and will answer them according to what is best for you.

How do you know? Because He is faithful in His love. And this psalm proclaims that faithful love with the special word *chesed* again. What do you learn about the lovingkindness of the Lord from verses 7, 16, and 21?

At the end of David's expressions of struggle, his cries for help, and his statements of faith in the Lord, there is a message to those around him. The title of this psalm is "For the choir director. A Psalm (song, melody) of David." The end of this song includes a charge to the assembly.

Based on David's testimony, what are we to do and to know according to Psalm 31:23-24?

While there was some uncertainty regarding whether or not David himself experienced the suffering described in Psalm 22, there is a key factor in Psalm 31 that indicates that this particular psalm was one of David's personal experiences. He says in verse 10: "my strength has failed because of my iniquity." David sinned. Jesus did not. But both David and Jesus turned to the Lord and trusted in His faithfulness during the extreme trials of their lives.

David is a model of someone just like us who lived by faith in the lovingkindness of the Lord. Jesus is the model of one, in flesh just like us, but without sin, who endured pain and suffering on our behalf, by faith in God. And so, as both Hebrews and Psalm 31 tell us – we too are to be strong, not grow weary, and not lose heart, but let our hearts take courage in the Lord as we endure trials through faith in the Lord.

Psalm Thirty-Two

David briefly mentioned something in the previous psalm which I think he expounds upon in the following psalm. He said "My strength has failed because of my iniquity, and my body has wasted away." (Psalm 31:10 [NAS]) This is something we should think about, and that is most likely the very purpose of the psalm we will study today. Psalm 32 is entitled a "maskil" which is usually understood to mean a "wisdom" psalm. Let's listen to the wisdom of David.

Please read Psalm 32.

Respond with your reflections, questions, prayers or praise.

_____

_____

_____

_____

How blessed! How happy! Do you remember how the first psalm began? "Blessed is the man...." And we saw that Psalm 2 ends with that statement as well: "how blessed are they.....". The book of Psalms began urging us to find our happiness in walking in the ways and words of the Lord and in finding refuge in His Son. By delighting in God's Word we find that we fall far short of His holiness. And so we see our sin and our need for forgiveness.

Let's walk through the different sections of this psalm, noting what David tells about his dealing with sin in his life.

Psalm 32:1-2: Cleansed from sin! How does David describe this and react?

Psalm 32:3-4: Concealing sin. What impact did this have on him?

Psalm 32:5: Confessing sin. What did David do?

Psalm 32:6-7: Counsel from David regarding sin. What is his instruction to us?

Psalm 32:8: <u>Counsel from the Lord regarding sin.</u> What is His encouraging promise?

Psalm 32:9-10: <u>More counsel from David.</u> What is the warning and what is the hope?

Psalm 32:11: <u>Celebration!</u> How are the forgiven described and what are they to do?

We must take sin seriously. David uses four different words to describe sin in the first two verses. Let's examine them.

Look up the definitions for the following words:

Transgression: Strong's #6588
Hebrew word:
Hebrew definition:

Sin: Strong's #2401
Hebrew word:
Hebrew definition:

Iniquity: Strong's #5771
Hebrew word:
Hebrew definition:

Deceit: Strong's #7423
Hebrew word:
Hebrew definition:

> These verses are an example of Hebrew poetic parallelism, since these four words are placed side by side and cover the entire spectrum of what sin is. Notice that David was tracking the downward progression of sin, first, as a rebellion against God and a revolt against His authority. Then sin is depicted as missing the way God has marked out for a man, a departure from righteousness. Then guilt overwhelms him and he becomes polluted within. Finally, man becomes self-deceived as he justifies his own sin to himself and he refuses to deal with its wrongness. [1]

The downward spiral of sin. It begins with the first act of rebellion against God. Rebellion sounds so extreme, doesn't it? But any disobedience is rebellion. And one thing leads to another, until we are deceived, and wasting away in sin.

You recorded above the impact that concealing sin had on David's life. Could you become physically or emotionally weak from hiding your sin today?

What happened to the Corinthians? Note what you learn from 1 Corinthians 11:28-32

Leon Morris, in his book <u>The Biblical Doctrine of Judgment</u> says: "the New Testament makes it clear that God is engaged upon a present activity of judging. Here and now, men may know that their actions are weighed by one Judge and action taken accordingly. These judgments are incentives to self-examination." [2] And he even says that "everywhere in the Bible, God's judgments are to incite men to self-examination and repentance."

What does Isaiah 1:18 say?

What does the Lord promise in Isaiah 43:25?

How do we receive this forgiveness according to Acts 2:38?

David said: "I acknowledged my sin to You; and my iniquity I did not hide…" and he confessed his transgressions to the Lord. We must recognize and admit our sins. The Holy Spirit will show us our sins, and we must agree with Him.

It's time for an examination under the light of the Holy Spirit. Is there any rebellion, wandering, uncleanness or perversion, or rationalization about sin that you have hidden in your heart? Acknowledge your sin, confess it, and go and sin no more. You will not be asked to share this with anyone.

Now please reread Psalm 32:1-2.

Rejoice in being cleansed from sin! Have you noticed that while David is very specific regarding the gravity of sin (using four different words), he is not specific regarding what his sins were. Keep this in mind… you can share God's amazing grace in your life without revealing the gory details of your sinfulness.

With a cleansed heart and spirit, David counsels others and the Lord counsels him. You noted this earlier. Please read the conclusion to this psalm once more – verse 11. But don't stop there, because, Psalm 33 is a song of celebration that the upright can sing!

Read Psalm 32:11 and Psalm 33, and rejoice in the Lord!

Arranging the Flowers

Psalm 33

This psalm is appropriately placed as the true response of one who has experienced the forgiveness of Lord as David did in Psalm 32. This is also a great national psalm anticipating the Lord's fulfillment of all of His promises, which He will do because of His faithful, covenant love (chesed – verses 18, 22). It is a great song of joy, with what seems to be four stanzas covering different topics – even as our hymns today do. It has an exciting introduction (1-3) and a comforting conclusion (20-22). One commentator has entitled it "A Hymn to the Creator" and sees the stanzas concerning: The Lord's Word (4-9), The Lord's Plan (10-12), The Lord's Eye (13-15), and the Lord's Might (16-19). [1]

Psalm Thirty-Four

We now encounter a poem (not a song) that continues the praise of the Lord that we've just seen in Psalm 33. This is an alphabetical poem – in Hebrew – with the first word of each verse beginning with the consecutive letters of the alphabet. The overall theme of fearing the Lord is covered from **aleph** *to* **tav**... *that's A to Z to you and me!*

Please read Psalm 34.

Respond with your reflections, questions, prayers or praise.

_____

_____

_____

_____

Did you notice the heading of this psalm? We haven't spent much time looking at the historical situations from which the psalms were written. It's an interesting thing to do, but, it isn't extremely important. Where other books of the Bible give us many details about people, places, and events, the Psalms rarely mention specific settings. And that is actually to our benefit. They can stand alone, apart from their historical setting, and be used for praise and prayer by all of God's people at any time.

But this psalm does give us information to consider. So let's examine David's story and see why the "editors" chose to remind us of this bit of Biblical history.

What details are given in the heading of Psalm 34? What did David do? Who is mentioned besides David? What happened to David?

Please read the account of this event in 1 Samuel 21:10 – 22:1. Note again – what did David do? And who is mentioned besides David? What happened to David?

Hmmm. We've almost got the whole story here. But did you notice a discrepancy in the names of the kings? Let me quote John Goldingay's summary for you to clear it up as best as we can.

> The heading links the psalm with an occasion when David had fled from Saul and taken refuge with a Philistine king, but then came to be afraid of that king. Fear is a rare experience for David, who normally is surrounded by others' fear and is a cause of it. In 1 Samuel the king is Achish of Gath, but introducing the name of Abimelech, king of Gerar, in the psalm reinforces the point, since he was an earlier Philistine king whom Abraham and Isaac also attempted to deceive because of their fear. (Gen 20, 26) Readers are thus encouraged to imagine how Abraham, Isaac, or David might have conquered fear by learning the lesson of this psalm, and/or how they might do something different with their fear. [1]

Please read through Psalm 34:1-11, and make notes of each phrase which includes "fear(s)".

Is the king of the Philistines mentioned at all in this psalm? Is David's fear of him referenced in the poem? Not at all! The message of this psalm is that we are to fear the Lord, not man, and trust in the Lord during all our times of trouble because He will deliver us.

If the Hebrew poets were conscientious about the precision of their work, and we assume they were, then the structure of this poem makes an important point. In the Hebrew, this psalm has 23 verses – our English has 22. In the Hebrew, the heading is counted as the first verse, and what we read as "verse 1" is "verse 2" in the Hebrew. So what?

If there are 23 verses, then what is obviously the central verse, the middle verse, the one upon which the whole poem balances?

      In the Hebrew: verse _____

      In the English: (Hebrew verse_____ minus one = _____)

      And what does that verse say?

Do you agree that this is the main point of this poem? Why or why not?

When we studied Psalm 23, I hope you learned that because the Lord is your Shepherd, there is no need to fear... because He is with you to protect you. (Ps 23:4) But now, we need to understand the right type of fear to have.

Please look up the definition for:

Fears (Psalm 34:4): Strong's #4035
Hebrew word:
Hebrew definition:

Fear (Psalm 34:7): Strong's # 3373
Hebrew word:
Hebrew definition:

Which one of the words and its definition is the one which should describe our fear of the Lord? (The answer is not "both of them!")

This psalm is written by one who lived in the fear of the Lord and trusted in Him for deliverance. How did he experience this according to Psalm 34:4-10? What example is there for us to follow? What promises can we expect to be fulfilled?

How does David "teach the fear of the Lord" in verses 12-14? How is the person who fears the Lord described?

I was surprised to find that the phrase "fear of the Lord" only occurs in a few of the books of the Bible. Note what you learn from the following:

2 Chronicles 19:4-9

Job 28:20-28

Psalm 111:10

Proverbs 8:13

Proverbs 14:26-27

Proverbs 16:6

Proverbs 19:23

Proverbs 31:30

Fearing the Lord and seeking refuge in Him was a very important point in the introduction to the book of Psalms.

Please summarize the exhortation in Psalm 2:10-12.

And now, reviewing your notes on "the fear of the Lord", explain this concept in your own words.

What does the Lord do for those who fear Him, according to Psalm 34:15-22?

Based on this passage, do you think that a Christian should be free from all troubles? Is that what this teaches? What should be our attitude regarding troubles, trials, and tragedy?

Even Jesus, who feared the Lord perfectly, experienced and endured suffering. I know we have already mentioned this in our studies. But this psalm points us to look at Jesus' death again, because the gospel of John quotes Psalm 34:20.

Please read John 19:31-37. How was Psalm 34:20 fulfilled?

Did the Lord fail to deliver Jesus from death? No. He delivered Him through death – to resurrection.

> John saw in this incident a foreshadowing of Jesus' ultimate deliverance and vindication. His unbroken bones were a reminder of God's commitment to the godly and a sign of things to come. Jesus' death on the cross was not the end of the story; God vindicated him, as John goes on to explain in the following context (John 19:38–20:18). [2]

Please read through this psalm in its entirety one more time, because there is one more thing I want you to see. Highlight, underline, or circle LORD, or Him (when referring to the LORD).

How often is the Lord referred to as David walks through the alphabet?

David has now taught us the blessing of fearing the Lord, based on his own experience. Psalm 34 was a poem, not a prayer. But Psalm 56 is a prayer to pray when we are afraid. Notice the heading, and conclude today's lesson putting all your trust in the Lord.

Psalm 56 [NAS]

FOR THE CHOIR DIRECTOR; ACCORDING TO JONATH ELEM REHOKIM. A MIKHTAM OF DAVID, WHEN THE PHILISTINES SEIZED HIM IN GATH.

1   Be gracious to me, O God, for man has trampled upon me;
Fighting all day long he oppresses me.
2   My foes have trampled upon me all day long,
For they are many who fight proudly against me.
3   When I am afraid, I will put my trust in You.
4   In God, whose word I praise,
In God I have put my trust;
I shall not be afraid.
What can mere man do to me?
5   All day long they distort my words;
All their thoughts are against me for evil.

⁶ They attack, they lurk,
They watch my steps,
As they have waited to take my life.
⁷ Because of wickedness, cast them forth,
In anger put down the peoples, O God!

⁸ You have taken account of my wanderings;
Put my tears in Your bottle.
Are they not in Your book?
⁹ Then my enemies will turn back in the day when I call;
This I know, that God is for me.
¹⁰ In God, whose word I praise,
In the LORD, whose word I praise,
¹¹ In God I have put my trust, I shall not be afraid.
What can man do to me?
¹² Your vows are binding upon me, O God;
I will render thank offerings to You.
¹³ For You have delivered my soul from death,
Indeed my feet from stumbling,
So that I may walk before God
In the light of the living.

Arranging the Flowers

Psalm 35

This is a call for the Lord to rise up and fight! The Lord is seen as a warrior who defends, protects, vindicates, and delivers His people. The Lord alone is salvation. Once again, we have an example of David calling on the Lord, trusting Him, and maintaining his righteousness before the Lord. "Stir up Yourself, and awake to my right and to my cause, my God and my Lord. Judge me, O Lord my God, according to Your righteousness, and do not let them rejoice over me." (Psalm 35:23-24 ^{NAS}) It seems appropriate that this psalm follows Psalm 34 where David turned from fear of man to fear of the Lord. It is an honest expression of one who is suffering from injustice done against him. It speaks on behalf of individuals of all times who have been violated, and reminds us to trust the Lord to carry out His justice on our behalf.

Psalm 36

The previous psalm encouraged the people to say "The Lord be magnified, who delights in the prosperity of His servant." (Psalm 35:27 NAS), and this psalm is recognized in its heading as being "of David the servant of the Lord." As Psalm 35 asked for the Lord's deliverance against his enemies, Psalm 36 petitions God to continue His protective love and to defeat the wicked. This psalm beautifully describes the character of God upon which the requests are based:

> 5 Your lovingkindness, O LORD, extends to the heavens,
> Your faithfulness reaches to the skies.
> 6 Your righteousness is like the mountains of God;
> Your judgments are like a great deep.
> O LORD, You preserve man and beast.
> 7 How precious is Your lovingkindness, O God!
> And the children of men take refuge in the shadow of Your wings.
> 8 They drink their fill of the abundance of Your house;
> And You give them to drink of the river of Your delights.
> 9 For with You is the fountain of life;
> In Your light we see light. NAS

Psalm Thirty-Seven

Why do bad things happen to good people? Why do good things happen to bad people? This poem – another alphabetical one – gives us wise counsel on how to wait on the Lord's judgment of the wicked who will eventually be destroyed, even though they seem to be "living the good life" right now. Patience is the virtue required from us.

Please read Psalm 37.

Respond with your reflections, questions, prayers or praise.

_____

_____

_____

_____

This is a long psalm isn't it! There are 22 letters in the Hebrew alphabet, and it seems that David had much to say with every letter. Every other verse begins with successive letters of the Hebrew alphabet. Remember, this is a poetic device to give a comprehensive teaching on a particular subject – in this case – patience.

I was introduced to a wonderful children's song about patience when as a teenager I babysat for my neighbor. Her little girl had a record (remember those?) that she played over and over, which was to my benefit because I learned the following song. Imagine a big, fat, slow snail singing in a deep voice!

> Have patience
> Have patience
> Don't be in such a hurry
> When you get
> Impatient
> You only start to worry
> Remember!
> Remember!
> That God is patient too
> And
> Think of all the times
> When others have to wait for you! [1]

What is the first instruction given to us in Psalm 37:1?

"When you get impatient you only start to worry..." Do not fret because of evildoers. This phrase is repeated several times. The verb is from a word that means to burn, or to let anger be kindled. The Hebrew literally says: "do not kindle yourself." Don't get heated up! Don't worry! Calm down! Those are trustworthy biblical exhortations.

Why shouldn't we worry? What does this psalm tell us?
Verse 2

Verses 7-10

Verses 12-15

Verse 17

Verse 20

Verse 34

Verse 38

Please return to the introduction to the book of Psalms and record what you learn about the wicked according to the following verses:

Psalm 1:4-6

Psalm 2:1-5

The stage is set. Those who do not turn from their wicked ways to the righteous ways of the Lord will perish in the Lord's wrath. Our God is a God of holiness and justice. But not worrying is easier said than done.

Are you experiencing an injustice in your life that is causing you to fret?

Instead of fretting, what are we to do when we see the wicked, ungodly, unrighteous prospering? This psalm gives us some of our most familiar and comforting verses. What are the commands given to us in the following verses?

Verses 3-8

Verse 27

Verse 34

These are clear commands, and they are the way to renew our minds when we are stuck in the worry mode. Which one of these instructions is most helpful to you right now?

What are the blessings that we will receive if we wait patiently for the Lord?

Verse 4

Verse 6

Verse 11

Verses 17-19

Verses 23-26

Verses 28-29

I want to follow the exhortations of this psalm so that I will enjoy those blessings. What about you? Let's examine a precious truth more closely and make sure that we understand it well.

In contrast to allowing negative feelings toward evildoers to control us, Psalm 37:4 tells us to do what? Please write out the entire verse.

The verb used in this verse is only used this way a few times in Scripture. How it comes to be translated as "delight" is a little bit confusing, so please take my word for it (based on my research) that it means "to take great pleasure in."

> The path to true self-fulfillment does not lie in a preoccupation with self but in selfless preoccupation with God. When the psalmist sets his heart on God, God reciprocates by making him truly fulfilled. [2]

How do the following verses describe delighting in the Lord?
Psalm 43:4

Psalm 94:19

Habbakuk 3:17-19

1 Peter 1:7-8

What is it about the Lord that makes you delight in Him?

And when we delight in Him, He gives us the desires – literally, the requests – of our hearts.

What do the following verses tell you about making requests of the Lord?
Psalm 145:19

John 14:13

John 15:7

1 John 3:22

1 John 5:14

Please take time to make your requests to the Lord right now. What are you asking Him for?

Note thy part and God's part. Do thou "*delight,*" and he will "*give.*" [3]

Delighting in the Lord, making your requests to Him, not fretting, being patient.... These are exhortations that the apostle Paul summarized beautifully in his letter to the Philippians:

"Rejoice in the Lord always; again I will say, rejoice! Let your forbearing spirit be known to all men. The Lord is near. Be anxious for nothing, but in everything by prayer and supplication with thanksgiving let your requests be made known to God. And the peace of God, which surpasses all comprehension, shall guard your hearts and your minds in Christ Jesus." Philippians 4:4-7 [NAS]

Please return to Psalm 37 and read the conclusion of this psalm. What is the hope for the blameless, upright man according to verses 35 – 40?

I hope that you have found comforting promises in the truths of this psalm. Everyday life can make us doubt the sure perspective of Scripture. This is a very valuable psalm, about which Charles Spurgeon says: "It is a Psalm in which the Lord hushes most sweetly the too common repinings of His people, and calms their minds as to His present dealings with His own chosen flock, and the wolves by whom they are surrounded." [4]

Luther closes his exposition of the psalm with the words, "Oh, shame on our faithlessness, mistrust, and vile unbelief, that we do not believe such rich, powerful consolatory, declarations of God, and take up so readily with little grounds of offence, whenever we but hear the wicked speeches of the ungodly. Help, O God, that we may once attain to right faith. Amen."

Arranging the Flowers

Psalm 38

This is a psalm of misery, because of sin, sickness, and snares. It has no turning point or relief, no word of comfort from the Lord, and yet because it is a prayer it shows the faith, hope and trust of David in his Lord. As he counseled in Psalm 37:34 "wait for the Lord and keep His way", so David declares in Psalm 38:15: "For I hope in You, O Lord; You will answer, O Lord my God." NAS

Psalm 39

This psalm sounds very similar to the previous one. David is afflicted, and he is silent… until he must speak. And so he asks the Lord to give him understanding of his days. He receives the perspective of his life from eternity's viewpoint. We need to remember how very short life is, because it will remind us that eternity is in view. This psalm needs to be in our repertoire of prayers, because many days will come when it will express our hearts – and help us to hope in the Lord. "Hear my prayer, O Lord, and give ear to my cry; do not be silent at my tears; for I am a stranger with You, a sojourner like all my fathers." (Psalm 39:12 NAS) While this psalm actually ends on a note of despair, it is followed in the next psalm by a testimony of the Lord's answer to the prayer.

Psalm Forty

This is a beautiful psalm with which I expect you are familiar. It seems to me to be like an azalea bush, with many blooms on every branch. This song (actually named as a psalm) moves from David's testimony to an exhortation to the assembly, to a review of God's faithfulness, to an expectation of His future deliverance, and ends with a plea from David for help in his current crisis. And in the middle, we'll find another passage that the author of Hebrews understood to be speaking of Jesus. Let's examine and enjoy this profusely blooming psalm!

Please read Psalm 40.

Respond with your reflections, questions, prayers or praise.

_____

_____

_____

_____

"Waiting, I waited." That's how the Hebrew puts the first words of this song. Isn't that just what the previous psalms were about? Waiting on the Lord?

What happened after David waited on the Lord? See verse 2.

That's vivid imagery of the difficult circumstances David had found himself in, which we've seen described in the past few psalms. Please review them and note the trials in following verses:

Psalm 34: heading, and verse 4

Psalm 35:4-7

Psalm 35:19-20

Psalm 37:7, 14

Psalm 38:3-5

Psalm 39:7-8

The slimy pit, one of mud and mire, which he was sinking in, describes a time of distress so horrible that there was no way for him to escape on his own. There were many times in David's life that he may have felt this way: he experienced adversity (1 Sam. 18:10-17, 23:15-29), family difficulty (2 Sam. 15-18), emotional distress (2 Sam. 18:19-33), and he committed grave sin (2 Sam. 11). Once again, we see that the psalm does not give explicit details of the trial, allowing us to relate to David in whatever type of trial we are experiencing. Do you feel trapped in a horrible pit right now? There is hope in the Lord.

From the mud to the mountain… the Lord put David on solid ground again. Then what? How did David respond and what did he expect? See verses 3 and 4.

Isn't this what the psalms have been teaching us? Please review once again and note what we've recently discovered:

Psalm 34:1-3

Psalm 34:11

Psalm 34:22

Psalm 37:5-6

Psalm 37:23-24

The first half of this song is one of thanksgiving – how does David continue to describe what the Lord has done? See Psalm 40:5.

When you've been in the pit, whether it was of your own making, or the sufferings that are a part of our lives on earth, and you are delivered out of it... do you sometimes feel like you can't even explain all that God has done? This is also the testimony of John as he ended his gospel: "And there are also many other things which Jesus did, which if they were written in detail, I suppose that even the world itself would not contain the books that would be written." (John 21:25 NAS) I agree! It's very difficult sometimes even to put into words the wonders that the Lord works in our lives. But would you please give it a try?

Write out a few of the wonders that God has performed in your own life. Make this a time of praise to Him.

Now we come to a portion of this song that speaks not about God's works, but about our works. What good works has David demonstrated? See verses 6-10.

David's good works are based on his understanding of what is most important to the Lord. We might initially think that this psalm indicates that the Lord did not want any sacrifices at all, in any way, shape or form. But that would be in conflict with the clear teaching of the Lord Himself that we find in the book of Leviticus. We should understand the statement in verse 6 to mean that the Lord is more concerned about obedience than He is about sacrifices. 1 Samuel 15:22-23 NAS supports this: "And Samuel said, 'Has the Lord as much delight in burnt offerings and sacrifices as in obeying the voice of the Lord? Behold, to obey is better than sacrifice, and to heed than the fat of rams.'"

I've asked you to look at this verse in a previous lesson, but it is so important to understanding verse 7 that I'd like you to see it again. What was the king instructed to do in Deuteronomy 17:18-20?

Fear the Lord. Delight in Him. Trust in Him. Obey Him. Are these directions beginning to sound familiar? Do you realize how often they are being repeated in the Psalms, whether in specifically repeated words or in general concepts? The scroll David speaks of in this psalm is probably the one he wrote for himself, as Deuteronomy instructed him to do.

We looked at several ways of delighting in the Lord in our last lesson, but there is another aspect that Psalm 40:8 reminds us of: "I delight to do Thy will, O my God; thy law is within my heart." Delighting in the Lord means delighting in His word and His will.

What do you learn from the following verses?

Psalm 1:2-3

Psalm 37:31

Psalm 112:1

Psalm 119:92

Mark 12:32-34

John 14:15

Even when we delight in the law of the Lord, we find ourselves falling far short of obeying it as we want to. (See Romans 7 for Paul's wrestling with this difficulty) After his declaration of his delight in the law of the Lord, David turns to the Lord in need for deliverance from his sin. The rest of the psalm is a prayer for help.

What are David's specific requests in verses 11-17?

As you look at this psalm as a whole, what can you learn about prayer? What was David's thought process?

I mentioned at the beginning of our lesson that Psalm 40 is quoted in Hebrews in reference to Jesus. Let's look at that passage.

Please read Hebrews 10:1-10.

What was the result of Jesus coming to do the will of the Father according to Hebrews 10:10?

What are the blessings of the sacrifice further explained in Hebrews 10:14-18?

Do you see how it all fits together? Psalm 40 shows us that obedience from the heart is better than legalistic sacrifices. And when we don't obey, we can turn to the Lord for forgiveness and deliverance. Hebrews shows us that the best sacrifice of all, made once for all time, for all men, was the death of Christ. His obedience to the Lord in giving of Himself as a sacrifice makes the way for men to receive the Holy Spirit, to have the law of the Lord written on their hearts, and to receive forgiveness of sin. There is great reason to declare God's wonders among the people!

"Let all who seek You rejoice and be glad in You;
Let those who love Your salvation say continually, 'The Lord be magnified!'"
Psalm 40:16 ^{NAS}

Arranging the Flowers

Psalm 41

This is the last psalm of Book I. It has 12 verses, plus one more that we refer to as the "doxology" which ends each of Book I, II, III, IV, and V. The theme of the last psalm is one of prayer from David, when sickness has overcome him and his enemies, even his friends, are hoping for his death. Once again, we see David turning to the Lord, who alone can deliver him from his suffering. "As for me, I said, 'O Lord, be gracious to me; heal my soul, for I have sinned against You.'" (Psalm 41:4)

The Doxology

"Blessed be the Lord, the God of Israel,
From everlasting to everlasting. Amen and Amen."
Psalm 41:12 ^{NAS}

In all that has been experienced in the life of David in the record of Psalms 1 – 41, the Lord has been faithful, powerful, his only hope, and the One who alone provides salvation. He is worthy of worship!

Book Two: Psalms 42 — 72
Introduction

We've seen David's name in the heading of all but two psalms in Book I. (Psalm 9 and 10 are considered to have originally been one psalm, and Psalm 33 is an appropriate response to Psalm 32). It's time to take a look at the authors of Book II. Getting a glimpse of what collections have been placed where reminds us that there was a purpose in the order of the psalms.

Please note the authors named in the headings for the psalms which comprise Book II.

Psalms 42 through 49 _____

Psalm 50 _____

Psalms 51 – 65 _____

Psalms 66 – 67 _____

Psalms 68 – 71 _____

Psalm 72 _____

Are these the only times that these authors are mentioned? Who are the authors of Book III?

Psalms 73 – 83 _____

Psalms 84 – 85 _____

Psalms 87 – 88 _____

Korah's story is related in Numbers 16:1 – 50. It's a fascinating account of one who wasn't happy with his assignment at the tabernacle. Korah's discontent ended in his death. But that wasn't the end of the story.

Who are the Sons of Korah? What do you learn about them from the following references?

During Moses' leadership:
Numbers 26:9-11

During King David's reign:
1 Chronicles 6:22, 31-32

During King Jehoshaphat's reign:
2 Chronicles 20:18-19

During King Hezekiah's reign:
2 Chronicles 31:14

What does this tell you about the dating of Psalms 42 – 49, 84 – 85, and 87 – 88? And for whom do you think they were written?

Once again, the actual historical setting of the psalms is hidden from us, and therefore we can apply them to any situation. We can learn though, the perspective of the nation of Israel from these psalms, as they were written for the community. Just as David as an individual could experience difficulties and trust in the Lord, so too could the nation experience difficulties and look to the Lord for His deliverance.

Psalms Forty-Two — Forty-Nine

Regarding Psalms 42 through 49, John Sailhammer states: "When read in sequence, a thematic development can be seen in the arrangement of the psalms." [1] *He makes the following connections:*

Psalm 42: begins with a plea for restoration and return to God's favor. "My soul thirsts for God, for the living God; when shall I come and appear before God?" Psalm 42:2 [NAS]

Psalm 43: continues the same line of thought – that of a castaway seeking to return to God's presence. "O send out Your light and Your truth, let them lead me; let them bring me to Your holy hill and to Your dwelling places." Psalm 43:3 [NAS]

Psalm 44: the complaint continues that God has rejected and humbled them, and ends with the call of the congregation for divine redemption. "Rise up, be our help, and redeem us for the sake of Your lovingkindness." Psalm 44:26 [NAS]

Psalm 45: the divine Redeemer comes as the King who is glorious and defeats the enemies of His people. "Gird Your sword on Your thigh, O Mighty One, in Your splendor and Your majesty!" Psalm 45:3 [NAS]

Psalm 46: Jerusalem, the King's city, is described at the time of His coming and His presence there means that there is no reason to fear. "God is our refuge and our strength, a very present help in trouble." Psalm 46:1 [NAS]

Psalm 47: God's reign as King from Jerusalem is portrayed as extending beyond His chosen people to include all the earth. "For the Lord Most High is to be feared, a great King over all the earth." Psalm 47:2 [NAS]

Psalm 48: Jerusalem at peace under God's protective care is described. "Beautiful in elevation, the joy of the whole earth, is Mount Zion in the far north, the city of the great King." Psalm 48:2 [NAS]

Psalm 49: With the last thought of Psalm 48 being that God will guide until death, this psalm provides the wisdom that the godly should not worry in the face of death. "But God will redeem my soul from the power of Sheol, for He will receive me." Psalm 49:15 [NAS]

I am once again faced with the very difficult task of choosing which psalms to spend more time on. I expect that most of the psalms above are familiar to you, and we would enjoy spending a day enjoying each one.

I think it would be a good idea right now for you to just read through the eight psalms of the Sons of Korah. Enjoy them one by one, and respond to the thought-provoking questions below.

Psalm 42 and 43 – Do you ask yourself questions about your spiritual condition? How can you overcome dark, dismal despair?

Psalm 44 – What place does suffering have in the life of the faithful believer?

Psalm 45 – Does your heart overflow with praise of your King? How often do you anticipate the coming of your Divine Bridegroom?

Psalm 46 – What do you need to do to "be still" – to cease striving, and know that the Lord is your sovereign God, in control of all of the circumstances of your life?

Psalm 47 – What is your favorite praise song to your King? How do you feel about clapping your hands for the Lord?

Psalm 48 – Great is the Lord - in every place. What setting prompts you to recognize His greatness and praise Him?

Psalm 49 – What will you leave behind, at the end of your life, that is of eternal value?

Psalm Fifty

Sometimes in an arrangement of flowers, there will be one stem that is unique that stands out from the rest and makes a striking statement. This psalm is like that.

We will enter the courtroom of the Lord today, where He is presiding as the true Supreme Court Judge. This psalm is a sober one that holds very important truths for us to grasp. It is placed here as a message to the nation of Israel – appropriately following the previous psalms of the Sons of Korah. And, it sets the stage for the confession found in Psalm 51.

Please read Psalm 50.

Respond with your reflections, questions, prayers or praise.

_____

_____

_____

_____

Asaph is recorded as the writer of this psalm. His role in worship is interesting and exciting. What do the following verses tell you?

1 Chronicles 16:1, 4-7, 37

2 Chronicles 29:30

Psalm 50 is a psalm of a "seer" – a prophet, and is very similar in its language and message to that of other prophets like Isaiah and Jeremiah.

It is composed of three parts. Briefly describe what is communicated in each of it's sections:

The Divine Summons (verses 1-6)

The Divine Speech (verses 7-15)

The Divine Sentence (verses 16-23)

Psalm 50:3 describes the way the Lord comes. How do the following references add to your understanding of this?

Exodus 19:18

Jeremiah 23:19-20

Nahum 1:6-7

> …this fire not only precedes Yahweh, as if you could relax once Yahweh passes, but whirls around on all sides. There is no safety zone. [1]

Who does the Lord call to stand before Him and be judged? How are they described according to Psalm 50:4-5 and 7?

Does the Lord rebuke His people for making improper sacrifices in verses 7-15?

*Commentators understand this passage to mean that the people were faithful in making sacrifices to the Lord, as they had been commanded, and they were not rebuked for that. However, they came to the wrong conclusion that the Lord **needed** the sacrifice of animals, as if for food for Himself.*

> It was common in the Mesopotamian context to consider sacrifice as service, through which humans fulfilled their obligation to provide the gods with three meals a day. For this reason, the great Sumerian scholar A. Leo Oppenheim [in his book on Ancient Mesopotamia] titled an important section on the sacrificial system "The Care and Feeding of the Gods." [2]

According to Psalm 50: 9-13, how does the Lord explain that He has no need of anything from us?

How do the following verses support this truth?
Genesis 1:1

1 Chronicles 29:11

Isaiah 42:5

Acts 17:24-25

The Lord's self-sustaining independence is a basic truth that we should never lose sight of. Sometimes, we make our God too small. When we begin to think of God as being like us, we've made a terrible mistake that will handicap our faith. The Mighty God, God, the Lord – needs no support system. But we desperately need Him to support and strengthen us.

Do you have the right perspective of your worship of the Lord? Why do you sing to Him and serve Him?

How does the Lord conclude His speech to His people? What does He want from them? (verses 14-15)

What does Leviticus 7:11-15 tell you about the thank offering (also called the peace offering) ?

Rather than dismissing actual sacrifices, the Lord invites His faithful people to give Him – literally – thank offerings. These were not just words of thanksgiving, but the actual offering of an animal. It symbolized fellowship with the Lord and was offered in thankfulness for a specific blessing, in keeping vows, and in general thankfulness to the Lord. When the people were in fellowship with the Lord through proper sacrifices, they would be able to call on Him and trust Him to answer their prayers.

How do you show your thankfulness to the Lord?

So far, the Judge who came in a consuming fire has corrected His people but has not convicted them of fault. The last section of this psalm presents the evidence of guilt.

According to Psalm 50:16-21, to whom does the Lord speak and of what does He accuse them?

In a word, these people were hypocrites! Their walk did not match their talk. Instead, they were walking, standing, and sitting with sinners. Does that remind you of Psalm 1? Instead of speaking out against them, they accepted them. The Lord did not rebuke His people for their worship, but rebuked them for their behavior. He will not accept right worship without right ways.

The Lord makes a shocking statement: "You thought that I was just like you!" Speaking of the Greeks, Aristotle said: "Men create gods after their own images, not only with regards to their form, but with regard to their mode of life." [3] Incredible! With this statement, the Lord addresses the behavior of men as well as the attitude of their hearts.

What is the truth about our God?
Deuteronomy 4:39

Isaiah 45:5-6

Isaiah 45:21-22

Is there anything in your attitude or behavior that indicates that you also have mistakenly thought that God is like you? Or that you are like God?

The verdict of the Judge is announced in the final verse: if there is no change, there will be destruction. And true worship is announced: honor the Lord with sacrifices of thanksgiving and live according to God's ways. Those who do will see the salvation of God.

What is the appropriate response to conviction of guilt? Repentance! Psalm 51 leads all who read it in heartfelt confession and hope for restoration of fellowship with the Lord.

"The Mighty One, God, the LORD, has spoken...." Psalm 50: 1 [NAS]

Psalm Fifty-One

You are probably familiar with this psalm, and you may have, as I have, turned to it for a pattern of confession during times of conviction. It is bittersweet, isn't it? Rather than being a bright cheerful flower, this psalm is one with its head weighed down with grief. But by the end of its prayer, its head will be lifted up in joy.

Please read Psalm 51.

Respond with your reflections, questions, prayers or praise.

_____

_____

_____

_____

What characteristics of the Lord are recognized in Psalm 51:1-9?

What condition does David recognize that he is in according to Psalm 51:1-9?

> Note the words used for sin here: transgressions means acts of rebellion, defying God by crossing over the line God has drawn; iniquity means inward crookedness, perversity; sin means missing the mark, failing to meet God's standard. [1]

What was the result of Adam and Eve's sin on the generations that followed them according to the following verses?

Genesis 6:5

Ecclesiastes 9:3

Jeremiah 17:9

Mark 7:20-23

Titus 3:3

After his confession, David makes requests for restoration of fellowship with the Lord. What does he want the Lord to do according to Psalm 51:7-12? List the actions he asks the Lord to take. (We will consider the results in the next question.)

David mentions hyssop which was used in different types of cleansing: being dipped in blood to consecrate the tabernacle, being dipped in blood to cleanse a leper, and being dipped in water to cleanse a tent where someone had died. David understood that his sin had defiled him and only God could cleanse him.

What would be the results of God's mercy and forgiveness according to Psalm 51:7-15?

David expresses the hope of the Lord's grace that we now understand more fully under the New Covenant. What was promised and fulfilled in these Scriptures?
Deuteronomy 30:6

Ezekiel 36:25-27

Matthew 26:26-28

Acts 1:4-5, 2:1-6, 11

2 Corinthians 5:17

What is the condition of your heart? Ask the Lord to give you wisdom to see the truth of your innermost being.

The joy of salvation and the forgiveness of sin, and the grace of God that sustains us day by day is worth opening our mouths about! Praise Him by telling others of His forgiveness, by singing joyfully of His righteousness and by declaring His praise.

The end of Psalm 51 reflects the heart of true worship which was the message of the previous psalm showing us that sacrifices were to be the offered from the heart with the right attitude and with right behaviors in day to day life. The specific sin of adultery was mentioned in Psalm 50:18, and the heading of Psalm 51 addresses David's sin of adultery. Remember that David lived during the time that the Levitical system of sacrifice was being carried out in obedience to the word of God. Sacrifices from David would not be acceptable to the Lord until he confessed his sin.

What type of sacrifices are appropriate to offer to the Lord according to Psalm 51:16-19?

Please look up the definitions for the following words:
Broken: Strong's #7665
Hebrew word:
Hebrew definition:

Contrite: Strong's #1793
Hebrew word:
Hebrew definition:

These are painful words. Have you recognized your sin in such a way that you have experienced their grief?

What do these Scriptures say about the words broken and contrite?
Psalm 34:18

Psalm 147:3

Luke 18:11-14

Please close today's lesson by re-reading through Psalm 51 — this prayer of confession, repentance, restoration, and rejoicing. If you have not yet made it your own prayer, please do so now.

> "...the sorrow that is according to the will of God
> produces a repentance without regret, leading to salvation..."
> 2 Corinthians 7:10 NAS

Arranging the Flowers

Psalms 52 — 60

Most bouquets need what we would call "filler", the greenery that gives the flowers a setting in which to shine. While I wouldn't dare call any of the psalms "filler", I do see these next psalms as being a part of the circumstances in David's life from which we learn and grasp the big picture, and then other psalms stand out a little more brightly.

Psalms 51 through 71 are all attributed to David except Psalms 66 and 67. They speak of the trials and the enemies that David encountered and show his steadfast trust in the Lord. Make notes on the circumstances given in the following psalms, and the statements of trust that are expressed in them.

Psalm 52
Circumstance (heading):

Trust (verse 1,8):

Psalm 53
Circumstance (verse 1):

Trust (verse 6):

Psalm 54
Circumstance (heading):

Trust (verse 4):

Psalm 55
Circumstance (verse 3):

Trust (verse 18):

Psalm 56
Circumstance (heading):

Trust (verse 4)

Psalm 57
Circumstance (heading):

Trust (verse 1):

Psalm 58
Circumstance (verse 1 – 2):

Trust (verse 11):

Psalm 59
Circumstance (heading):

Trust (verse 16):

Psalm 60
Circumstance (heading):

Trust (verse 12):

Psalm Sixty-One

Psalm 61 sums it all up in song. A desperate prayer. A powerful hope. It shows us that David knew the Lord as his safe and secure refuge. There is no better shelter than the Lord Himself. How many songs do you know praising the Lord as your Rock?

Please read Psalm 61.

Respond with your reflections, questions, prayers or praise.

_____

_____

_____

_____

This song has two stanzas. The first is a request (Psalm 61:1-4), and the second is an expectation (Psalm 61:5-8).

Psalm 61:1-3: Why is David calling on the Lord? (The previous psalms gave us many circumstances to consider.)

Psalm 61:2-4: What does David need?

Several different images are used to describe the protection and security of the Lord. Please look up the definition for the following words:
Rock (Psalm 61:2): Strong's #6697
Hebrew word:
Hebrew definition:

Refuge (Psalm 61:3) : Strong's #4268
Hebrew word:
Hebrew definition:

Shelter (Psalm 61:4): Strong's #5643
Hebrew word:
Hebrew definition:

These words help us grasp the safety and protection that we can find in the Lord. So too does the image of finding shelter under "His wings." These are all poetic images to help us picture the Lord who is invisible and completely different from anything in His creation. We are reading the Bible literally which means we are reading it according to the type of literary devices that are used. The Lord is not a rock with wings.

Biblical references to the wings of birds are common, especially in Psalms, many of them exquisitely poetical. Often the wings of an eagle are mentioned because they are from 7 to 9 feet in sweep, of untiring flight, and have strength to carry heavy burdens: so they became the symbol of strength and endurance. [1]

Some commentators have suggested that the image [of wings] may have been further associated with the wings of the cherubim that overarched the ark of the covenant in the Most Holy Place of the tabernacle or temple. In this case the protective wings of Yahweh might become effective when one flees to the temple and seeks asylum there. [2]

Both of these explanations of the "wings" of the Lord make sense and would communicate strength and safety, but I have witnessed the protection provided by a mother killdeer, a brown bird with black and white rings around her neck. She made her nest in a pile of mulch in an island in the church parking lot. Four big brown speckled eggs were visible as my family walked by. Rather than flying away, she stayed put, guarding her eggs, and spreading her wings out to protect them. That demonstrated Psalm 61:4 to me!

David was not the first to understand that the Lord was a Rock and a Refuge. Note how the following verses describe the Lord:
Genesis 49:24

Deuteronomy 32:4, 11, 15

Ruth 2:12

Do you run for cover under the shelter of His wings only when there is a time of trouble? How can you keep yourself dependent on the Lord's protection at all times?

In the second verse of his song, what did David expect and why (Psalm 61:5-8)?

David makes a few very amazing statements –

    Let me dwell in your house _____ "(Psalm 61:4)

    He [the king] will abide before God _____...(Psalm 61:7)

    So I will sing praise to Your name _____, (Psalm 61:8)

What was David thinking?! How could this be fulfilled? Well, the Lord actually did promise this to David. We just need to understand which king verse 7 was talking about.

What did the Lord promise to David in 2 Samuel 7:12-13?

According to 2 Samuel 7:18-19, 28-29, how did David respond?

Based on the verses above, we can understand that while David is praying for himself, he also includes prayer for the king who is to come and be established on the throne forever. David expected the Lord to fulfill His promises in the Messiah. Until He came, it was reasonable for David to pray that he would live a long life himself.

Are you waiting for the King to come? What are you doing while you're waiting?
What should you do? Note the exhortations from the verses below:
2 Thessalonians 2:1-2

2 Timothy 4:1-2

Titus 2:11-14

In the midst of terrible times when we are desperate for a safe place, we can find security in the presence of the Lord and in His plan. Those who have trusted in Christ as Savior have a blessed hope. Even when we are crying and we are fainthearted, we can praise the name of the Lord.

David will continue to call upon the Lord who is his Rock and seek refuge in Him in the psalms to come. Close today's lesson with David's words from Psalm 62.

Psalm 62:5 -8 NAS

5 My soul, wait in silence for God only,
For my hope is from Him.
6 He only is my rock and my salvation,
My stronghold; I shall not be shaken.
7 On God my salvation and my glory rest;
The rock of my strength, my refuge is in God.
8 Trust in Him at all times, O people;
Pour out your heart before Him;
God is a refuge for us.
Selah.

Psalm Sixty-Three

Have you ever been in a desert, where it is dry and dusty and the only plants are tumbleweeds and cacti? God made the cactus just for the desert, and although there is very little water, it is a succulent plant and some varieties even bloom. This psalm is like a cactus flower – a blossom in the desert. The heading tells us that David was in the Judean wilderness, which doesn't have tumbleweeds and cacti, but does have rugged terrain with brown mountains – and not much else. However, the desert in Israel would be extremely fertile if it only had water.

Before you read Psalm 63, I'd like you to read one of the accounts (there are several) of a time David when was in the wilderness, hiding from his enemies. Remember Psalm 61 and 62 and David's cries for refuge.

How did God deliver David in 1 Samuel 23:14-29? And what was he assured of in verse 17?

Please read Psalm 63.

Respond with your reflections, questions, prayers or praise.

_____

_____

_____

_____

This is a song! Of longing, but of faith. "O God. You are my God." There is no doubt that God is, and that he is David's God.

How does David express his desire for the Lord in Psalm 63:1?

Please look up the definition for:
Seek (Psalm 63:1): Strong's #7836
Hebrew word:
Hebrew definition:

Whether your Bible translation includes the idea of "seeking early" or not, that is a fundamental aspect of the word used. There is an indication of acting with effort and commitment by rising early. What is expressed is an earnest, eager desire for the Lord.

What type of behavior in your life shows that you are eagerly seeking the Lord?

> When the bed is softest we are most tempted to rise at lazy hours; but when comfort is gone, and the couch is hard, if we rise the earlier to seek the Lord, we have much for which to thank the wilderness. [1]

Rejoice in the promise that the Lord gives in Proverbs 8:17 "I love those who love me; and those who diligently seek me will find me."

Look at Psalm 63:2-8 and list what David has experienced from the Lord and what his responses are:
Experiences   **Responses**

When we read the story of David's life, we see more hardship than happiness. If we only read the praise portions of his psalms we will have a skewed view of his life. He had terrible troubles! How could he say, in the midst of them: "Your lovingkindness is better than life?" David, the man after God's own heart, did not preach a prosperity gospel. But he did proclaim that the Lord was faithful and loving, strong and mighty, and worthy of all of his adoration for all of his days, even in the worst of days.

Psalm 63:5 is especially interesting to note in light of David's opening statement. "My soul thirsts for You, my flesh yearns for You.... My soul is satisfied as with marrow and fatness, and my mouth offers praises with joyful lips." NAS *Several translations have "will satisfy", indicating anticipation of future blessing, but based on the Hebrew, I agree with other translations which have the present tense as I have quoted above.*

How can you be satisfied with the Lord, with who He is and with what He has done in the past when you are desperately longing for Him in the present?

How does Lamentations 3:17-25 provide an example of this?

David shifts from talking about how the Lord helps Him to how the Lord will handle his adversaries. This is another aspect of his confidence and satisfaction in his God.

What will happen to his enemies according to Psalm 63:9-11?

How did David know that? Let's look at some history for the answer:
In Exodus 15:3-8, what happened to Israel's enemies - Pharaoh and his army?

In Numbers 16:28-33, what happened to Moses' "enemies" - Korah, Dathan, and Abiram?

In 1 Samuel 17:45-47, 50-51, what happened to David's first "enemy"?

In 1 Samuel 26:7-11, what did David say when presented with an opportunity to kill Saul? And what happened to Saul in 1 Samuel 31:3-4?

Romans 12:19-21 ^{NAS} Never take your own revenge, beloved, but leave room for the wrath of God, for it is written, "Vengeance is Mine, I will repay," says the Lord. "But if your enemy is hungry, feed him, and if he is thirsty, give him a drink; for in so doing you will heap burning coals upon his head." Do not be overcome by evil, but overcome evil with good.

As I mentioned earlier, this psalm is like a cactus flower, blooming in the desert, in the harshest of environments. It's a beautiful song of confidence, but one that it may take us time to learn to sing with all our heart.

Please read through Psalm 63 in its entirety and pray that you too will seek the Lord and be satisfied with Him no matter what you are going through.

Arranging the Flowers

Psalm 64

"Hear my voice, O God, in my complaint…" etcetera, etcetera, etcetera! Life is up and down for David. But he keeps turning to the Lord. An especially important expectation shows up in this psalm which links it to the next - David knows that *all* men will fear the Lord when He has overcome His enemies. (Psalm 64:9) As so many of David's complaints do, this psalm ends on a positive note which echoes Psalms 1 and 2: "The righteous man will be glad in the Lord and will take refuge in Him; and all the upright in heart will glory." (Psalm 64:10)

Psalm 65

After the dryness of the desert wilderness in Psalm 63, the water flowing through this psalm is refreshing! It first tells us that *all* men will come to the Lord, He brings them near His courts, and they are satisfied. God is the Savior who is also the Sustainer: "You visit the earth and cause it to overflow; You greatly enrich it; the stream of God is full of water; You prepare their grain, for thus You prepare the earth." (Psalm 65:9) Is this history or prophecy? It's just a matter of when you read it. For us, it's both. It ends with the meadows and valleys shouting for joy… a shout that continues in Psalm 66!

Psalm 66 and 67

These are both anonymous songs in between David's psalms. Together they tell us that God delivered Israel out of bondage to testify of His salvation and invite all nations to be blessed by Him.

Psalm 66:1 - 5 ^{NAS}

For the choir director. A Song. A Psalm.

Shout joyfully to God, all the earth;
Sing the glory of His name;
Make His praise glorious.
Say to God, "How awesome are Your works!
Because of the greatness of Your power
Your enemies will give feigned obedience to You.
"All the earth will worship You,
And will sing praises to You;
They will sing praises to Your name."
Selah.
He turned the sea into dry land;
They passed through the river on foot;
There let us rejoice in Him!
He rules by His might forever;
His eyes keep watch on the nations;
Let not the rebellious exalt themselves.

Psalm 67 ^{NAS}

For the choir director; with stringed instruments. A Psalm. A Song.

God be gracious to us and bless us,
And cause His face to shine upon us— *Selah.*
That Your way may be known on the earth,
Your salvation among all nations.
Let the peoples praise You, O God;
Let all the peoples praise You.
Let the nations be glad and sing for joy;
For You will judge the peoples with
Uprightness and guide the nations on the earth.
Selah.
Let the peoples praise You, O God;
Let all the peoples praise You.
The earth has yielded its produce;
God, our God, blesses us.
God blesses us,
That all the ends of the earth may fear Him.

Psalm Sixty-Eight

Do you know "The Star Spangled Banner?" Do you know when it was written, what all the words mean and what the song is describing? It's all about the American flag, has words we don't use everyday and was written during the War of 1812. But we can sing it with passion and patriotism any time, right? The 4ᵗʰ of July, the beginning of baseball games, a presidential inauguration. It strikes a deeper chord however when we are at war. My point is that even though the song was written and sung during a specific event, it still is appropriate and moving at other times. The song of Psalm 68 is like that. So pull out your palm branches and wave them in praise to the greatness of the Lord.

Please read Psalm 68.

Respond with your reflections, questions, prayers or praise.

_____

_____

_____

_____

I really wanted to include this psalm in our study, and when I finally decided that I would – the first commentary that I read said "the difficulties of interpreting Psalm 68 are almost legendary!" [1] *So if you were a little bewildered in trying to understand what you just read, you are in good company. There are more than fifteen words and expressions that we will find nowhere else in the Bible. That's okay. It's a beautiful song celebrating Lord's victory and triumphal entry up to Mount Zion from which He will rule all the earth.*

> David probably wrote this psalm when he conquered the holy city Jerusalem (2 Sam. 5:6-9) or when he moved the ark of the covenant from the house of Obed-Edom to Jerusalem (2 Sam. 6). Appropriately this psalm would have been used at subsequent victories of Israel, leading the people to rejoice in God for the victory He gave to His people. This inspired hymn reviews the history of Israel from their leaving Mount Sinai, through their wilderness wanderings, to their entrance into and conquest of the Promised Land. [2]

That's the past. But the Lord is coming back and once again will defeat His enemies and ascend to Mount Zion in victory to rule over all the ends of the earth. Don't forget the future!

COME, LET US WORSHIP

In Psalm 68:1-6, list the ways that God carries out His conquests.

What are the contrasts between the wicked and the righteous?

In this same section, what characteristics of the Lord are described?

In Psalm 68:7-14, again list the ways that God carries out His conquests. Verses 7-10 probably refer to the time in the wilderness of Sinai, and verses 11-14 to the victory over Canaan.

Describe the manifestations of the Lord's power and glory recorded in the following verses:

In the wilderness of Sinai:
Exodus 19:18

Exodus 24:15-17

In the Promised Land:
Joshua 10:5, 8-11

Judges 5:1-5

In the future against Gog and Magog:
Ezekiel 38:18-23

In the future at the Battle of Armageddon:
Revelation 16:16-21

The battle belongs to the Lord! When the Lord provided victory, He gave the Israelites the spoils of war (Psalm 68:12). The land received rain (Psalm 68:9), the people slept safely at night (Psalm 68:13), and the women spread the good news (Psalm 68:11). That makes sense! There is no clear consensus on what the "wings of a dove covered with silver and pinions with glistening gold" refers to! It's a beautiful image though, and that is the point of the section. The success of God is glorious!

Now we will look at the place the Lord chooses to call His home. It will be helpful for you to know that Mount Hermon, with its height of 9000 feet, is the grandest mountain in the area of Bashan. Bashan was the area where fat cows and strong bulls were raised and it was the home of fierce lions. It was a symbol of that which was lofty, rich, and powerful.[3] It is probably Mount Hermon, of Bashan, that is personified in these verses.

How is the dwelling place of the Lord described in Psalm 68:15-18?

What else do you learn about the mountain of the Lord from these Scriptures?
Deuteronomy 33:2

Isaiah 2:2

Ezekiel 40:2, 43:1-2, 7

Joel 3:17

Micah 4:1-2

Zechariah 8:3

Mount Zion today is quite a contested territory. It is in Jerusalem, but is under the control of the Palestinians and the gold-domed Al-Aksa Mosque sits there. The Lord will return one day and prove that it belongs to Him. Prophecy explains that there will be a great earthquake and Mount Zion will rise up, becoming higher and grander than those mountains around it! (Zechariah 14:4 – 10)

The song of praise continues in Psalm 68:19-23. Record what you learn in the two categories on the next page.

Psalm 68:19-23

How the Lord is described	How His enemies are described

It will be much more pleasant to think about the Lord's goodness to us than the gory details of war. These are precious truths which are echoed throughout the Scriptures and upon which we can depend.

How does the Lord care for you day by day?

The Brooklyn Tabernacle Choir sings a song in which the Lord reminds us of His daily attention to our lives.

Didn't I wake you up this morning
Weren't you clothed in your right mind?
When you walked on this problem,
Didn't I step in right on time?
When you got weak along life's journey,
My angel carried you…
So you would know just how much I love you

Didn't I put food on your table
Show up!...when the bills were due
When the pains were racking your body
Didn't I send healing down to you
When you were lost in sin and sorrow
I died to set you free
So you would know just how much I love you [4]

The Lord was victorious over sin and death! He loves us so much. Now we are ready to celebrate in the procession! The King is coming!

What's happening in Psalm 68:24-27? Who is in the parade?

"Oh when the saints... go marching in.... oh when the saints go marching in... Oh Lord, I want to be in that number, when the saints go marching in!" I would love to have been in the parade or a part of the cheering crowd as this procession ascended Mount Zion. I am so looking forward to heavenly celebrations! Look back at the prophecy of Ezekiel 43 on page 116.

Do you cheer at football games? Graduations? Concerts? Kindergarten plays? Would you please <u>not</u> just sit there right now, but stand up and praise the Lord? Psalm 68:26 tells you to do just that.

There are two more stanzas of this song of celebration. Hang in there. Don't miss the big ending!

According to Psalm 68:28-31, what do the people want from God and for God?

The author of "The Star-Spangled Banner" understood that victory comes from the Lord and included it in his song. I didn't know that our national anthem included the following stanzas of praise:

Oh! Thus be it ever when freemen shall stand
Between their loved home and the war's desolation
Blest with victory and peace, may the Heav'n rescued land
Praise the Pow'r that hath made and preserved us a nation
Then conquer we must, when our cause it is just,
And this be our motto, "In God is our trust."
And the star-spangled banner in triumph shall wave
O'er the land of the free and the home of the brave. [5]

And now, praise the Lord! Read Psalm 68:32-35. What do these verses tell you about our God?

Our God is awesome, isn't He? I hope you have seen His power, glory, and majesty in the lesson today. He is the triumphant King who reigns on high in heaven right now, and will reign on earth one day. Blessed be God!

Arranging the Flowers

Psalm 69

What mourning and grief, trials and suffering are expressed through this prayer. But once again, in the midst of suffering, faith in God stands out. "Answer me, O Lord, for Your lovingkindness is good; according to the greatness of Your compassion, turn to me, and do not hide Your face from Your servant, for I am in distress; answer me quickly." (Ps. 69:16 – 17 [NAS]) The question is – what is this prayer doing here immediately after the anthem of praise in Psalm 68? This one is by David, and like the previous psalm, looks forward to God's fulfillment of His promise to establish His kingdom in Zion. This psalm expresses the misery that David and the nation are experiencing while they wait for the King to come.

Psalm 69 is distinctly messianic, as it finds its ultimate fulfillment in the coming of the Lord Jesus Christ. One of the most quoted psalms in the New Testament, it was applied by the apostles to the rejection suffered by Christ. From this psalm we see a foreshadowing of our Lord's persecution by the world (v. 4; cf. John 15:25), zeal for God (v. 9; cf. John 2:17), and circumstances of the cross (v.21; cf. Matt. 27:48). From this prophetic vantage point, we learn in this psalm that Christ is the perfect embodiment of righteousness that was persecuted by evil men for doing God's will and God's work. Likewise, all believers today who live godly lives in Christ Jesus will suffer persecution (2 Tim. 3:12). [1]

Psalm 70

Come quickly, Lord! That's the urgent plea of this short psalm – which is identical to the last verses of Psalm 40. It is possible that it was placed here, a second time in the psalter, because its urgent cries so appropriately restate the requests of Psalm 69. By itself, it's a model prayer for us – short – intense – and eager. In the context of Psalm 69, 70 and 71, it becomes a cry for God to set up His universal Kingdom and send His eternal King – soon!

Psalms 71 and 72

We are coming to the close of Book II. You will see that the two psalms at the end of this book are strategically placed. Psalm 71, while not given a title in the Hebrew text, is attributed to David in the Septuagint (Greek Old Testament) and seems to be the prayer of an aged man. Psalm 72 is either by Solomon or for him. In either case, the psalm is a prayer for the son of the king. David's reign was coming to an end, and the heir to the kingdom would soon be seated on the throne.

Psalm Seventy-One

Let's see what someone who has lived a long life of faith in God has to say.

Please read Psalm 71.

Respond with your reflections, questions, prayers or praise.

_____

_____

_____

_____

Please highlight, circle or underline the phrases which show indicate the age of the psalmist. (You will need a total of 4 different colors to complete all the highlighting exercises in this lesson.)

Psalm 71 ^{NAS}

¹ In You, O LORD, I have taken refuge;
   Let me never be ashamed.
² In Your righteousness deliver me and rescue me;
   Incline Your ear to me and save me.
³ Be to me a rock of habitation to which I may continually come;
   You have given commandment to save me,
   For You are my rock and my fortress.
⁴ Rescue me, O my God, out of the hand of the wicked,
   Out of the grasp of the wrongdoer and ruthless man,
⁵ For You are my hope;
   O Lord GOD, You are my confidence from my youth.
⁶ By You I have been sustained from my birth;
   You are He who took me from my mother's womb;
   My praise is continually of You.
⁷ I have become a marvel to many,
   For You are my strong refuge.
⁸ My mouth is filled with Your praise
   And with Your glory all day long.

9   Do not cast me off in the time of old age;
    Do not forsake me when my strength fails.
10 For my enemies have spoken against me;
    And those who watch for my life have consulted together,
11 Saying, "God has forsaken him;
    Pursue and seize him, for there is no one to deliver."

12 O God, do not be far from me;
    O my God, hasten to my help!
13 Let those who are adversaries of my soul be ashamed and consumed;
    Let them be covered with reproach and dishonor, who seek to injure me.
14 But as for me, I will hope continually,
    And will praise You yet more and more.
15 My mouth shall tell of Your righteousness
    And of Your salvation all day long;
    For I do not know the sum of them.
16 I will come with the mighty deeds of the Lord GOD;
    I will make mention of Your righteousness, Yours alone.

17 O God, You have taught me from my youth,
    And I still declare Your wondrous deeds.
18 And even when I am old and gray, O God, do not forsake me,
    Until I declare Your strength to this generation,
    Your power to all who are to come.
19 For Your righteousness, O God, reaches to the heavens,
    You who have done great things;
    O God, who is like You?
20 You who have shown me many troubles and distresses
    Will revive me again,
    And will bring me up again from the depths of the earth.
21 May You increase my greatness
    And turn to comfort me.

22 I will also praise You with a harp,
    Even Your truth, O my God;
    To You I will sing praises with the lyre,
    O Holy One of Israel.
23 My lips will shout for joy when I sing praises to You;
    And my soul, which You have redeemed.
24 My tongue also will utter Your righteousness all day long;
    For they are ashamed, for they are humiliated who seek my hurt.

Do you see anything that might indicate that he is past middle age? Does he seem concerned about growing older?

Once again, we see a prayer for rescue from the wicked. Using a second color, highlight the phrases in Psalm 71 that are requests of the Lord for refuge, safety, deliverance, etc. How would you summarize the situation of the psalmist?

That gives us the setting, the circumstances of the psalmist. This is an older man, probably David, who is somehow being threatened by his enemies. There's something to be learned just from observing that situation.

Does life get easier? Should you expect problems to disappear as you grow older?

I don't see a man regretting his life, or one who is distressed about the choices that he made that have brought difficult consequences upon him. I see a man who has trusted in the Lord through all of his life, who is calling for help in the present, and who is even praying for the years to come to be filled with praise to the Lord.

Using a third color, highlight every occurrence of a name of the Lord in Psalm 71. How does this man address the Lord?

Please look up the definitions for the following words:
LORD (Psalm 71:1): Strong's # 3068
Hebrew word:
Hebrew definition:

God (Psalm 71:4): Strong's #430
Hebrew word:
Hebrew definition:

Lord (Psalm 71:5): Strong's #136
Hebrew word:
Hebrew definition:

GOD (Psalm 71:5):Strong's # 3069
Hebrew word:
Hebrew definition:

Which one of the names of God does this man use most often in this psalm?

> The word Elohim here is the very first term or name by which the Supreme God has made himself known to the children of men. (Gen.1:1) [1]

In Psalm 42 through 89 (Book II and Book III), the name Elohim is used more often than the name Yahweh.

> [Elohim] is the sole object of adoration; ... the perfections of His nature are such as must astonish all those who piously contemplate them, and fill with horror all who would dare to give His glory to another, or break His commandments; ... consequently He should be worshipped with reverence and religious fear; and every sincere worshipper may expect from Him help in all his weaknesses, trials, difficulties, temptations, etc.,; freedom from the power, guilt, nature, and consequences of sin; and to be supported, defended, and saved to the uttermost, and to the end. [2]

The psalmist calls on God according to every way that he knows Him. His God is the self-existant One who is eternal. His God is the Supreme Being over all of the universe and worthy of praise. His God is the Holy One of Israel, the God of the nation.

Please read through this psalm again and with a fourth color, highlight, then record below, how God is described. Also observe – which characteristic of God is mentioned more than any other?

Because of his knowledge the Lord's supremacy and holiness, in addition to this older man's plea for deliverance, he also makes several requests regarding what he wants to be able to do continually, for the rest of his life. What does he say in the following verses?

Psalm 71:3

Psalm 71:6

Psalm 71:8

Psalm 71:14

Psalm 71:15

Psalm 71:24

What do you learn regarding old age from the following Scriptures?
Psalm 48:14

Psalm 92:12 -15

Proverbs 20:29

Isaiah 46:3-4

2 Corinthians 4:16

Titus 2:2-5

This psalmist was not the only one who recorded words as he looked toward the last years of his life. Please read 2 Timothy 4:6-18.

How did Paul describe his present circumstances?

How did he describe the life he had lived?

What did he expect in his future?

Is there any indication that he has "retired" or is he still in active service to the Lord?

What do you pray for regarding your future? What is your outlook on serving the Lord in your old age?

> Wisdom doesn't automatically come with old age. Nothing does - except wrinkles. It's true, some wines improve with age. But only if the grapes were good in the first place. [3]

Before we leave this psalm, I'd like you to notice an idea that is going to show up quite often in the Book III – Psalms 73 – 89.

What does Psalm 71:17 say?

The same wording for "wondrous deeds" is used in Psalm 72, 75, 77, 78 (four times!), 86, 88, 89. It shows up in other psalms as well, but in a concentrated amount in this section of the psalter. We'll consider more about God's wondrous works in the lessons to come.

Until then, what wondrous things have you seen God accomplish throughout the days your life?

Psalm Seventy-Two

Are you familiar with edelweiss? It's a little white flower that grows in the mountains of Switzerland and other European countries. We're going mountain climbing today, so I'm thinking of it. I know of no better description of the psalm we are about to read than that of Dr. Steven J. Lawson. The following excerpt is taken from his introduction to Psalm 72 in the Holman Old Testament Bible Commentary.

Two towering mountain peaks rise up from the surrounding plains. One is immediately before you, close and near; the other looms on the horizon. A considerable distance separates the two peaks, causing the second to appear smaller. But as you approach them, you realize that the second peak is not the smaller of the two but actually larger. In fact, the closer you get to the peaks, the more the second peak towers over the first. The second mountain rises up into the clouds and disappears; the first remains easily in full view. The second peak is snowcapped; the first is not. The closer you draw to the two peaks, the more it becomes obvious; the grandeur of the second mountain far exceeds the first.

This is the dual effect presented in Psalm 72. Two towering mountain peaks of truth stand before the reader in this psalm. Each summit represents the reign of a mighty king. One is near and great; the other is far away yet even more grand. The first is the reign of Solomon who ruled over Israel; the second is the reign of Christ who reigns over all the earth. The first kingdom is temporal; the latter is eternal. The first is regional; the latter is universal. The first is the son of David, Solomon; the latter is the Lord Jesus Christ, a greater Son of David than Solomon. [1]

Please read Psalm 72.

Respond with your reflections, questions, prayers or praise.

_____

_____

_____

_____

This psalm is a prayer for the king, written by the king. So, he is praying for himself, but this also becomes a prayer for the Messianic King and a description of His reign. First, we will consider how this reflects Solomon's reign which is in itself a majestic mountain.

What did Solomon request for the king in Psalm 72:1-5?

What did Solomon request for himself in 1 Kings 3:7-14? What did the Lord promise him?

The story of two women in dispute over a baby that belonged to one of them immediately follows the account of Solomon's prayer for wisdom (1 Kings 3:16-27). Solomon's discernment regarding to whom the child belonged gave evidence that he had truly received wisdom from the Lord.

What does 1 Kings 3:28 tell you about Solomon and his wisdom, and the people's response?

In Psalm 72:5-7, how is the king's reign described? How long does it last?

We can easily understand the beautiful poetry regarding the sun – which shines day after day, and the moon – which lights up the sky night after night. But it's harder for me to understand how the king can "come down like rain upon the mown grass." We have to remember how critical rain was to the land. Rain was a blessing from the Lord that provided crops of fruit and grain. The leadership of the king was to be as refreshing and satisfying as the rain, bringing prosperity to the people.

We're already starting to see that the mountain in the distance is grander than the one we've begun to climb. How could an earthly king reign forever?

What was promised to David by the Lord in 1 Chronicles 17:11-14?

Does this answer our question? Would there be an earthly king who would rule forever? We have the vantage point in history to see that every son of David who sat on the throne eventually died. And we also have been given the grace to see Jesus – the King of the Jews – who died, but lives again! Revelation 19:11-16 tells us that the King of Kings is going to return to the earth, and Revelation 20:4 tells us that Christ will reign on earth for one thousand years. His kingdom will not come to an end through His death though. It will just undergo a universal makeover (Rev. 21), and He will reign for eternity, just as the Lord promised David.

How is the territory of the kingdom described in Psalm 72:8-11?

What territory did the Lord promise in the following verses?
Genesis 15:18

Exodus 23:31

Joshua 1:4

What territory did Solomon have dominion over according to 1 Kings 4:21-24?

Something is missing in those descriptions... oh, it's the "ends of the earth!" Solomon did have rule over a vast region, but, there's a more magnificent mountain in view. The Messiah will rule over all the earth. The psalms have been mentioning this idea and the frequency increases toward the end of Book II; you can find the phrase in Psalms 59, 65, 66, 67, 68, 69, and 72.

Note the phrases that indicate the dominion of the Messianic King.
Psalm 2:8

Psalm 22:27

Psalm 65:5

Psalm 67:2, 4, 7

Now let's look ahead. It has been announced that the King will rule over the entire earth forever. What do the following verses say?
Zechariah 9:9-10

Luke 1:31-33

Hallelujah! I praise the Lord that the day is coming when His perfect King will rule over all the earth and there really will be peace on earth! It's what the angels told us!

> "Glory to God in the highest, And on earth peace, goodwill toward men!"
> Luke 2:14 [NKJ]

Does Jesus Christ have dominion over you? What does it look like in your life? Do you have peace under His perfect authority?

What does Psalm 72:12-14 tell you about the kindness of the king?

If this is how the king treats others, should you do any less? How do you help the needy, afflicted, and weak?

What does Psalm 72:15-17 tell you about the blessings for and from the king?

Blessings For the King   **Blessings From the King**

Have you received blessings from the King? What are some of them?

What blessings does Ephesians 1:3-7 say that those in Christ have received?

When you are a subject of the King of Kings, He pours out His riches on you! There are many beautiful descriptions of the blessings that will come when Jesus Christ reigns on earth. Isaiah has much to say about Him who is the King – the Servant of the Lord. I hope these familiar verses will be understood even more as we read them with Psalm 72. They further describe the glorious mountain which in the future Millennial Kingdom will be the place of King's throne.

Summarize how the King and His kingdom is described in the following passages.
Isaiah 9:1-7

Isaiah 11:1-9

Isaiah 60:1-22

Would you please pray through Psalm 72, asking the Lord to answer the requests you are making on behalf of His King? Pray that all the earth will come to know Jesus as their King.

Psalm 72 concludes with a doxology which is the conclusion to this section of the book of Psalms, but also so appropriate for the psalm itself.

What are the specific connections in Psalm 72:18-19 to the rest of Psalm 72?

From Psalm 42 through Psalm 72, the wondrous works of the Lord have been magnified through prayers, poems, poetry, and praise. He rescues those in danger from their enemies, He comforts the weary, He makes His presence known, He demonstrates His lovingkindness which is better even than life. God's name has been exalted in these psalms and His glory has been on display. The whole earth should be singing His praises today. One day, it will. But we don't have to wait. What other response can we have, except to join in this worship of our God through whom was given the Savior, who is the reigning King?

Amen, and amen.

Arranging the Flowers

"The prayers of David the son of Jesse are ended."
Psalm 72:20 NAS

We have a special note here added by the editor. At some point, there was probably a collection of psalms by David that stood alone, and when that group was combined with other psalms, it was appropriate to add this note. All of Book II (Psalms 42 – 72) could have been attributed to David because – remember – the Sons of Korah were made worship leaders under David's administration. Their psalms could have been considered "David's" as well. If we look back to Book I (Psalms 1 – 41), we'll remember that all but four psalms were entitled "of David", so the statement that we find at the end of Book II is an appropriate summary of both books. And then other psalms and collections were added to complete the Psalter as we now know it, which is why we will see David again, as the author, in fourteen more psalms out of the remaining seventy-seven.

Those are the details. Now for the signifigance. What impact should this statement have on the interpretation of the entire book of Psalms? It's a hard thing to do, but if we step back and look at the forest (where we have found the flowers!), instead of just looking at the flowers, we will see that all of Psalms 3 – 72 are to be read as prayers regarding the Messiah – the Anointed King who was promised in Psalm 2. The prayers show the faith of David and the nation of Israel, through the good times and the bad, as they wait for their King to deliver them. And they show that they are delighting in God's word, expecting blessing, as promised in Psalm 1. How blessed is the man whose delight is in the law of the Lord! (Ps. 1:1-2) How blessed are all those who take refuge in Him! (Ps. 2:12) The Word of God and the Son of God. These are our only hope. There is no other way – but to trust and obey.

Book Three: Psalms 73—89
Introduction

Seventeen psalms make up Book Three. That's not very many, compared to the 41 psalms of Book 1, and the 30 psalms of Book Two. Here's the structure of Book Three based on the authors of the psalms:

Psalms 73 – 83 – by Asaph
Psalms 84 and 85 – by the Sons of Korah
Psalm 86 – by David
Psalm 87 and 88 – by the Sons of Korah
Psalm 89 – by Ethan the Ezrahite

I know you know David, and you've already learned something about Asaph and the Sons of Korah. Does it really matter whether you know anything about the authors or not? Well, God did record their names here, so, He wanted you to know. He has His reasons! Keep in mind that these were the worship leaders for the nation of Israel. And David as king was to be an example of a godly worshipper. Most of these psalms expressed the faith of the people as a whole, rather than that of an individual. They are grouped together in Book Three because they all reflect the struggle to trust God and hope in Him in the midst of the destruction of Jerusalem and the exile.

Book Three describes a defining moment in the history of the nation of Israel and the crisis of faith that the people experience. Their desperation, their memory of God's faithfulness and power, and their hope for restored fellowship in His presence is captured in this series of psalms. When we read them, we will be directed to remember Who God is and to remember His faithfulness. This book in the psalter is a perfect place to turn when we ourselves are experiencing a crisis of belief.

Psalms Seventy-Three — Seventy-Six

It's a little difficult to get an overview of seventeen psalms, but that's what we're going to try to do! Not all in one lesson though. For today - read through the following four psalms and make observations of what they express.

Please read Psalm 73 in its entirety and then answer the following questions:
What is the truth stated in verse 1?

What is the problem in verses 2-3?

What is the wrong perspective in verses 12-14?

What is the right perspective in verses 15-20?

What is the encouraging truth remembered in verses 21-28?

Please read Psalm 74 in its entirety. Notice and mark each occurrence of "Your" when referring to God, as well as the noun that it modifies (i.e. "Your inheritance").

What is the problem that this psalm begins with in verse 1?

A watershed event is described in verses 3-9. What happened that drastically impacted the faith of the nation of Israel?

What is the concern in verses 10-11?

What is the true perspective in spite of circumstances in verses 12-17?

On what basis does the psalmist call upon God to act according to verses 18-23?

Look back at your notes from reading Psalm 73. What must be remembered from Psalm 73 and applied during the crisis of Psalm 74?

Please read Psalm 75 in its entirety.
Verses 2-5 are the words of the Lord and verses 6-10 are the psalmist's comments.

How does the Lord answer the most pressing question of Psalm 74:10 – "How long…?"

What is the expectation of this psalm?

That was a quick overview of Psalm 75. Now we will consider Psalm 76.

Psalm 76 celebrates the judgment of the Lord having taken place, which was expected in Psalm 75. If the Lord judged His enemies in the past, He will do so in the future. This is the outlook of Psalm 76. And so, while it is a celebration of God's victory, it is also a statement of faith that He will be victorious again and all should fear him.

Please read Psalm 76 and consider the following outline. Summarize the truths from the psalm for each point.

- Verses 1-2: Eternal Truth

- Verse 3 :Review of God's Victorious Judgment in the Past

- Verse 4: Eternal Truth

- Verses 5-6: Review of God's Victorious Judgment in the Past

- Verses 7: Eternal Truth

- Verses 8-10: Review of God's Victorious Judgment in the Past

- Verse 11: Appropriate Response to God in the Present

- Verse 12: Preview of God's Future Judgment

So far, we've seen:
Psalm 73 – of Asaph – an individual's perspective corrected, which prepares the reader to to have the proper outlook during the problem of Psalm 74
Psalm 74 – of Asaph – a nation's concern over God's rejection and the timing of His judgment
Psalm 75 – of Asaph – an answer from God regarding the time of His judgment
Psalm 76 – of Asaph – a review of God's judgments in the past which gives hope for the future and prompts the proper response to Him today

That sets the stage for the remainder of Book Three. Israel must learn to be obedient to the Lord and trust Him even in the midst of difficulty and painful experiences. Our lives are just like theirs.

Please read through Psalms 73 through 76 again. What truths or perspectives do you need to believe during times of tragedy, heartbreak, and disappointment?

> As he that fears God fears nothing else, so he that sees God sees nothing else. [1]

In our next lesson, we will spend time looking at one of the most heart-wrenching cries to the Lord in the psalms (Psalm 77), and we'll look at the wisdom declared in response to the anguish expressed (Psalm 78).

Psalms Seventy-Seven — Eighty-Three

We must look at Psalm 77 and 78 side by side. The first is an introduction to the second. Together they point out what we need to remember when we are experiencing broken-heartedness, feelings of abandonment, and crisis. When our friends and family are sick, or have experienced a death – we often send flowers. With these two psalms the Lord offers a bouquet of white roses to give peace and perspective to hurting souls.

How does the psalmist express his grief in Psalm 77:1 – 4?

I expect that at some time you have experienced the depths of pain that are described here. The important question is – did your voice "rise to God?" Did you cry aloud? Do you turn to the Lord and   express your greatest sorrows to Him?

Asaph says that he considered the days of old (verse 5), and he remembered his song (verse 6). Asaph remembered what God had done in the past, and he remembered how he had sung praise to Him. But those memories only made Him more confused, because it seemed to him now that God had failed to keep His promises.

What six questions did Asaph ponder about the character of God?

These were certainly the reflections of the community of Israel as they experienced the destruction of Jerusalem and the Babylonian captivity. And they are questions that we ask at times as well. Someone has said that we should never doubt in the darkness what God has told us in the light. It's okay to ask hard questions, but our minds must focus on the truths that we know about the Lord.

What does Asaph determine to do in Psalm 77:11-12?

And when he does that – what does he declare about God through the rest of the psalm?

Psalm 77:13-20 is a very brief summary of the great things God had done for Israel and how He showed His power and love. It was the right thing to think on. But to combat doubt and hopelessness, we may need a more detailed description of what the Lord has done. That's what we find in the next psalm. Psalm 78 is a long, detailed account recording the works of God on Israel's behalf. It is worth the time it will take to read it – especially if you find yourself asking some of Asaph's questions from Psalm 77.

What is Asaph's introduction to Psalm 78 according to verses 1-4? How does he describe what he is about to say and what his purpose is?

The first wondrous work of the Lord is recorded in verses 5-6. What was it and what was its purpose?

Now – I'm not going to ask you about all 72 verses of this psalm! But, I do want you to read them. Psalm 78 reminds its readers that God is powerful and faithful and acts on behalf of His people. It also reminds us that the people of God did not respond to Him obediently whether they were blessed or stressed. This becomes a powerful parable for all times. Remembering God is the key to faithfulness and forgetting God is the key to failure, but God is faithful to His Word even when we fail. The point of the parable: Don't forget God like your fathers did!

Please read Psalm 78. Notice the contrasts between God's work and the people's responses.

The last wondrous works of the Lord are described in verses 65-72. What were they and how are the Lord and His people described?

Let's skim the surface of the next several psalms to see how they fit in the big picture of Book Three… the nation's crisis of faith and how they should respond to the Lord in the midst of their despair.

Please read Psalm 79 in its entirety, then fill in the blanks below.

The lament is that the nations have invaded God's _____.

The questions are _____? _____?

_____?

The request is that God would not _____ of their fathers, but would show compassion.

The cry is: Help us _____, for the glory of Your name, and

_____ and _____ for Your name's sake.

And then the people, the _____, will give

thanks to God forever; to all generations they will tell of His praise.

Do you think that Psalm 79 is an appropriate sequel to Psalm 78? Why or why not?

Psalm 80 continues with prayers for help and salvation, showing faith in the Lord who will be faithful to His people....

> Oh, give ear, Shepherd of Israel,
> You who lead Joseph like a flock;
> You who are enthroned above the cherubim, shine forth!
> "O LORD God of hosts, restore us
> and cause Your face to shine upon us,
> and we will be saved.
> Psalm 80:1, 19 NAS

And then in Psalm 81 and 82, the Lord speaks in judgment, explaining that if only His people would listen and obey, then they would be delivered.

> Hear, O my people, and I will admonish you;
> O Israel, if you would listen to Me!
> Oh that My people would listen to Me,
> That Israel would walk in My ways!
> I would quickly subdue their enemies
> And turn My hand against their adversaries.
> Psalm 81:8, 13,14 NAS

> God takes His stand in His own congregation;
> He judges in the midst of the rulers.
> Psalm 82:1

Psalm 83 is the last of the psalms of Asaph, with a final cry for God to act against His enemies.

> Let them be ashamed and dismayed forever;
> And let them be humiliated and perish
> That they may know that You alone,
> Whose name is the LORD,
> Are the Most High over all the earth.
> Psalm 83:17 – 18 NAS

I wonder if you feel like we are spending a lot of time with the psalms that are in Book Three. I do. But, the reason is that as a whole, they express the crisis of faith that the nation experienced, and we as individuals can learn from how they cried out to the Lord and how the Lord answered them and corrected their perspectives.

I asked you at the beginning of this lesson if you cry to the Lord – aloud – and express your grief to Him. Is there anything in this lesson that has been a surprise or an adjustment to your perspective on circumstances in your life?

How would you summarize the prayers that we've looked at today?

Psalms Eighty-Four — Eighty-Nine

In today's lesson, we will complete our overview of the remaining psalms of Book Three. The last six continue in the theme of the crisis of faith, but you may think that Psalm 84 doesn't quite fit. In the 1990's this psalm became the basis for a praise song and we probably associate it more with joy than with sorrow. It is however, actually a song expressing the longing of the Israelites for the temple of God.

Please read Psalm 84 in its entirety. I've have included a translation that I think best expresses the entire meaning of the psalm, but you may also enjoy reading it in a version that you are more familiar with.

PSALM 84

FOR THE CHOIR DIRECTOR; ON THE GITTITH. A PSALM OF THE SONS OF KORAH.

¹   How beautiful is Your dwelling place,
O Yahweh Sabaoth!
²   My soul yearns – even wastes away –
for the courts of Yahweh;
my heart and my flesh cry out to the living God.
³   Even a bird finds a home, and a swallow a nest for herself,
where she can put her young near Your altars, O Yahweh Sabaoth –
my King and my God –
⁴   How blest are those who dwell in Your house,
who can continually praise You! *Selah.*
⁵   How blest are those whose strength is in You,
with pilgrim-ways in their hearts!
⁶   Those passing through the Valley of Baca will make it an oasis;
moreover the early rain will clothe it with blessings.
⁷   They will go from strength to strength
till each appears before God in Zion.

⁸   O Yahweh Sabaoth!
Hear my prayer; give ear, O God of Jacob.
Selah.
⁹   Behold our shield, O God,
And look at the face of Your anointed.
¹⁰   How much better is a day in Your courts than a thousand others!
I choose waiting at the threshold of the house of God
more than dwelling in the tents of wickedness.
¹¹   For Sun and Shield is Yahweh – God;
grace and glory, Yahweh bestows;
He withholds no good thing from those who walk in integrity.
¹²   O Yahweh Sabaoth! How blest is the one who trusts in You. ¹

What phrases throughout this psalm indicate the desire to be in the temple of the Lord and in His presence?

Psalm 84:5 — 7 communicate a very important outlook that would have been a message to those devastated over the destruction of the temple and those in exile. It becomes an important message to us as well.

The "Valley of Baca" is probably the name of an arid valley through which pilgrims to Jerusalem would have traveled. "Baca" may have been the name of a plant found in the valley, but because this word is almost identical to the Hebrew word for "weeping" (bakhah), some understand the Valley of Baca to be a "valley of weeping" or "valley of affliction".

What does Psalm 84:5-7 tell us to do, to expect, and to depend on?

What names and descriptions of God are used in this psalm?

From Strong's Concordance, #6633, "Sabaoth" means: a mass of persons (or figurative things), especially regularly organized for war (an army); by implication a campaign, literally or figuratively (specifically hardship, worship): appointed time, (+) army, (+) battle, company, host, service, soldiers, waiting upon, war (-fare).

I have always understood Lord Sabaoth to mean Lord of Hosts, or Lord of the armies of heaven. But I have just learned from further research that Sabaoth also indicates (as noted above) a group of persons in some service to God, even in worship. The root word means to fight or to serve. The following comment is interesting: "No doubt service for Yahweh is seen as involving total dedication and careful regimentation, and since God is Yahweh of hosts, enthroned between the cherubim housed inside the tent of meeting, work associated with the tent may be considered spiritual war." [2]

The meaning of Yawheh Sabaoth in this psalm, given the theme of the psalm, is probably a recognition of the Lord as God over the servants of His temple. The Sons of Korah were gatekeepers – guardians if you will – of the temple grounds. They and all others who were in the service of leading worship were guardians of God's holiness. What greater warfare is there than to stand on the Lord's side, declare your allegiance to Him, and defend His reputation and glory? Even in and especially in the midst of the most difficult times.

Do you worship the Lord and defend His reputation during times of spiritual warfare and crisis? How?

It's hard to leave Psalm 84. But moving on is important, because if the Israelites want to return to the temple, they'll have to be restored in relationship to the Lord. This is the plea of Psalm 85.

> Restore us, O God of our salvation,
> And cause Your indignation toward us to cease.
> Will You be angry with us forever?
> Will You prolong Your anger to all generations?
> Will You not Yourself revive us again,
> That Your people may rejoice in You?
> Show us Your lovingkindness, O LORD,
> And grant us Your salvation.
> **Psalm 85: 4 – 7** [NAS]

Following the two psalms from the Sons of Korah is another psalm of David. It's the only one in Book Three. And then it will be followed by three final psalms from the Sons of Korah. David stands out once again as an example of a faithful follower of the Lord. Psalm 86 is the prayer of an individual, and it's insertion in the midst of the psalms of the community is to remind us that we are people of God as a whole congregation, but each of us must have a personal relationship with our Lord.

Psalm 86 is beautiful, rich, and full of critical truths. We'll pause just long enough to breathe in the fragrant aroma of this flower.

Please read Psalm 86. Write out the verse that is most meaningful to you.

Affliction. Adoration. Appreciation. Anticipation. This psalm has it all. David is dependent on the character of the Lord and His abundant lovingkindness. Let us all follow his example.

When we depend on the Lord, and trust Him as David did, then we will have hope for what He will do in the future. The next psalm captures this hope. The Sons of Korah have shown their longing to return to the temple (Psalm 84), to be restored in relationship(Psalm 85), and now to rejoice in the rebuilt city (Psalm 87).

Glorious things are spoken of you, O city of God.
....of Zion it shall be said, "This one and that one were born in her;"
and the Most High Himself will establish her.
Then those who sing as well as those who play the flutes shall say,
"All my springs of joy are in you."
Psalm 87:3, 5, 7 NAS

There is hope, but the desperate times continue. Whether we consider the circumstances of the Israelites in 586 B.C. (first destruction of the temple and exile), or in 70 A.D. (second destruction of the temple and dispersion), or in 1945 (the Holocaust), or in the recent years of the 21st century, we will see the chosen people of God suffering under persecution and prejudice, hostility and horrors of war. The nation of God is still waiting for Him to deliver them. And our lives can mirror theirs. We go through long, drawn-out, painful circumstances, waiting for God to deliver us. Psalm 88 expresses this dark, dreary, almost deadly despair.

O Lord, the God of my salvation,
I have cried out by day and in the night before You....
For my soul has had enough troubles,
And my life has drawn near to Sheol....
You have put me in the lowest pit,
In dark places, in the depths....
My eye has wasted away because of affliction;
I have called upon You every day, O LORD;
I have spread out my hands to You....
O LORD, why do You reject my soul?
Why do You hide Your face from me?
You have removed lover and friend far from me;
My acquaintances are in darkness....

Psalm 88:1, 3, 6, 9, 14, 18 NAS

Psalm 88 has no resolution, no word from the Lord that soothes the pain. It's called the saddest psalm of the entire Psalter. But it is a prayer to the Lord, indicating that even in the midst of the extreme, unending anguish and unanswered prayers, one must cling to God and persevere in faith.

How are you strengthening your faith right now so that when you are in the most extreme situations, you will be able to persevere through them by faith in God?

The last psalm of Book Three expresses the question one encounters when he has faith in God and in His promises, but God doesn't seem to be keeping His promises. The fact is that God is true to His word, even when we can't understand His plan. Psalm 89 is a reflection on the Davidic covenant, but brings the book of Psalms at this point to a dead end.

What is anticipated in Psalm 89:1-2?

Why is that anticipated according to Psalm 89:3-4?

The promise given is an overwhelming, wondrous work of God and prompts all of heaven, earth, and those on earth to praise Him! This is described in verses 5-18.

What are some of the highlights of this adoration of the Lord?

Two important points are made about the king – the kingdom – the throne. God will establish it based on His covenant with David… but notice the truths declared:

Righteousness and justice are the foundation of _____ throne;
Lovingkindness and truth go before _____. (Psalm 89:14)

For our shield belongs to the _____,
And our _____ to the Holy One of Israel. (Psalm 89:18)

What does this tell you about the kings of Israel and their throne?

Psalm 89:19-37 describes the incredible details of the Davidic Covenant. Please read through this section. What does God guarantee in verses 33-37?

That was the promise. But the present circumstances were in direct contrast to its fulfillment. The psalmist says "But You have cast off and rejected, You have been full of wrath against Your anointed." (Psalm 89:38 NAS) Wow. What a shock.

What does Psalm 89:39-45 tell you about the king, the covenant, the throne?

If you want to read the sad, historical accounts of this destruction, you can turn to 2 Kings 25 or Jeremiah 39. Ezekiel 21:26-27 NAS prophesies about the account this way: "thus says the Lord GOD, 'Remove the turban and take off the crown; this will no longer be the same. Exalt that which is low and abase that which is high. A ruin, a ruin, a ruin, I will make it. This also will be no more until He comes whose right it is, and I will give it to Him.'" The throne will be no more, until the One comes to whom the throne and crown truly belong. It's a dead-end, until a new way is made.

So what does the psalmist say as he sees the end of the kingdom, while remembering the promises of the covenant? How do verses 46-51 conclude this psalm?

No resolution. No answer from God. But, Book Three has one more statement and one more lesson to teach us.

What is the doxology in Psalm 89:52?

Is it more praise, less praise, or the same praise as the doxologies at the end of Book One (Psalm 41:13) and Book Two (Psalm 72:18-19)?

It reminds me of Job's praise to the Lord after the death of his children and servants and the destruction of all of his flocks and belongings. In his grief, he did not sin or blame God. "The Lord gave and the Lord has taken away. Blessed be the name of the Lord." Job 1:21 NAS

In spite of the confusion about the promises of God, and God's plan, and the destruction all around, and the removal of the throne of Israel, the psalmist can say "Blessed be the Lord forever!" This is a sacrifice of praise.

What are the circumstances of your life? How will you praise the Lord, declaring His greatness, no matter what?

As I was writing these lessons on Book Three and Israel's crisis of faith, I encountered my own crisis, disappointment, and grief. God didn't answer prayers the way I thought He would. These psalms have been expressions for my sorrow and direction for my soul.

I hope that the time you've spent in Psalms 73 – 89 will familiarize you with Book Three so that you can turn to it on your own during times of doubt and despair.

Blessed be the Lord our God forever. Amen.

Book Four: Psalms 90— 106
Introduction

In Book One and Two, the psalms established that those who delight themselves in the word of God and obey it, and those who seek refuge in the Son of God and fear Him will be blessed. The many trials of David and his cries for help proved that the Lord was faithful to protect, comfort, and deliver His people. The psalms have also established that the Lord promised an everlasting dynasty for David and he will always have a descendent on the throne. Many psalms gave evidence to the greatness of that kingdom: the city of God was described as glorious, victories were won, and the king was on the throne.

But it all came to an end in Book Three. And now the Davidic dynasty seems to be over. Forever? Book Four in Psalms shows that the people have come to a new realization. They have no earthly king, but they have realized that the Lord Himself is their King and their refuge. The psalms that make up the fourth book of Psalms praise the Lord God Almighty and highlight His incredible, incomprehensible attributes.

Book Four begins with the one and only psalm attributed to Moses. With the despair of Psalm 88 and 89 and the questions of "how long, O Lord?" and "where are Your former lovingkindnesses?" we are looking for answers. We find them from the wisdom of Moses in Psalm 90.

Psalm Ninety

Please read Psalm 90.

Respond with your reflections, questions, prayers or praise.

_____

_____

_____

_____

The question in Psalm 89:46 was: "How long, O Lord? Will You hide Yourself forever?" The answer given in Psalm 90 is not exactly what we would expect, but it does give us wisdom to adjust our perspective. Psalm 90 tells us much about the Lord's timing.

How long has the Lord been our dwelling place?

How long is one thousand years before the Lord?

How long is man's life?

How long does the psalmist want to be satisfied with the Lord?

Our life on earth takes on a completely different time frame when considered in the light of eternity. We must remember this whenever we are waiting on God to act. It's interesting that this psalm takes us back to the "beginning of time" as we know it, with several inferences to Genesis.

Record the parallels in the verses below.

Creation:
Genesis 1:1

Psalm 90:2

Curse of Sin:
Genesis 3:19

Psalm 90:3

No Sin is Secret:
Genesis 3:9-13

Psalm 90:7-8

Man's mortality is directly related to Adam's original sin. God decreed physical death so that mankind would not be trapped in a state of sin-stained flesh forever. Genesis 3:22-23 [NAS] *says: "Then the Lord God said, 'Behold, the man has become like one of Us, knowing good and evil; and now, he might stretch out his hand, and take also from the tree of life, and eat, and live forever'— therefore the Lord God sent him out from the garden of Eden, to cultivate the ground from which he was taken."*

How does Psalm 90 view man's short life according to verses 7-10?

Psalm 90:11-12 offers a message for all as we contemplate the brevity of life. What is the real problem? And based on that problem, what should our response be? Please take time to ponder these two verses.

> Now is the time to ask God for wisdom to become better students and stewards of our time and opportunities. We number our years, not our days, but all of us have to live a day at a time, and we do not know how many days we have left. A successful life is composed of successful days that honor the Lord. [1]

On the next page, you will find a chart depicting the days and hours of our lives. Why don't you do a quick review of how you are spending your time each day? (The chart begins early for the early birds and goes late for the night owls! You should get more than 5 hours of sleep!)

	Sunday	Monday	Tuesday	Wednesday	Thursday	Friday	Saturday
5:00am							
6:00am							
7:00am							
8:00am							
9:00am							
10:00am							
11:00am							
12:00pm							
1:00pm							
2:00pm							
3:00pm							
4:00pm							
5:00pm							
6:00pm							
7:00pm							
8:00pm							
9:00pm							
10:00pm							
11:00pm							
12:00am							

What are your priorities based on your current schedule and lifestyle?

Are these what you want your priorities to be? Are there any changes you would like to make? Take time to prayerfully consider your activities and responsibilities.

If you don't plan your time, someone else will. You have the responsibility of setting priorities based on the gifts, calling, and abilities that God has given you so that you will be able to spend your time wisely. Pray that the Lord will teach you to do so.

Reflecting back on Psalm 89 again, we will remember that another question asked was: "where are Your former lovingkindnesses, O Lord?" The rest of Psalm 90, and then Psalm 91 and 92 address this concern.

What is the prayer request in Psalm 90:13-17?

All of Psalm 91 reflects the lovingkindness and protection given from the Lord during one's whole life. What verse or verses are most meaningful to you today?

Because of the lovingkindness of the Lord, the life of the faithful will flourish. This is the declaration of Psalm 92. Please read Psalm 92 and note its reasons for praise to the Lord.

It is good to give thanks to the Lord and to sing praises to His name, isn't it?! It's so refreshing to praise the Lord with joy for what He has done. We've been struggling along through the trials of the Israelites, and we know they aren't over yet, just as the trials of our own lives are not over until we see Jesus face to face. But praising the Lord is soothing, encouraging, and uplifting to our souls. I look forward to praising Him more in the next lesson. We are going to see God the King high and lifted up!

Psalms Ninety-Three — Ninety-Nine

These seven psalms are arranged like a brilliant display of exotic, extraordinary flowers – multi-colored Bird of Paradise, Green Midori Anthurium, Red Ginger, White Dendrobium Orchids, and Purple Dendrobium Orchids. Most commentators see Psalms 93 through 99 as a unit of psalms with the theme being the Kingship of Yahweh. We are going to worship the Lord in all of His glory as we look at how He is described in these psalms.

Please read through each psalm, and record the characteristics of the Lord that are described. Briefly note the phrase, and try to summarize what you learn about the Lord. Make sure to note the different names of God that are mentioned. Sometimes, you'll just note His description. (You won't find a description in every single verse.) There will be repeated characteristics throughout these seven psalms; please record the repeats. They will show you what is emphasized about our God. This will be the main activity of our lesson, so enjoy the revelation of the Lord. The title of our study comes from Psalm 95 – so... Come, Let us Worship!

For example:
Psalm 93:1 – ' the Lord reigns' – He is King
'clothed with majesty' – He is majestic
'girded with strength' – He is strong

Psalm 93

Psalm 94

Psalm 95

Psalm 96

Psalm 97

Psalm 98

Psalm 99

Please look over the lists you have just made. What descriptions or characteristics are repeated the most often?

For the nation of Israel who is without their Davidic king (as expressed in Psalms 73 – 89), and for us today who cannot physically see our Savior King – what is the perspective that we gain from these psalms?

Did it surprise you to see how often the Lord was praised as "Judge" (Psalms 94, 96, 97, 98)? Why is this important?

Throughout these psalms, there are important statements about the word of God. The King is to be obeyed. Note what you learn from the following verses:

Psalm 93:5

Psalm 94:12-13

Psalm 95:7b-11

Psalm 99:6-8

Let's make sure that we observe and follow the exhortations that we find in these psalms! Our great God is worthy of all the enthusiasm and exaltation that we can give Him. What are we told to do in the following verses?

Psalm 95:1-2

Psalm 95:6

Psalm 96:1-3

Psalm 96:7-9

Psalm 97:10, 12

Psalm 98:4-6

Psalm 99:9

Our English "o come let us sing unto the Lord" is too tame for the text. The psalm opens with a crash of words. The Psalmist calls upon his hearers to shout and sing aloud.

We've been given the instruction, the permission, and the privilege of praising God! It sounds exciting to me – does it to you? And there is a wide range of expression of worship described in these verses. Are there a few words that you've heard before but don't quite know what they mean? Ascribe simply means give. Give God the glory, not anyone else. Exalt means to lift up. Lift up the Lord, hold Him in high esteem.

Please take all of the instructions into consideration. Our posture and our praise should reflect who we are and who God is.

> The phrase "bow down" means "to prostrate oneself," especially before a superior, although it is rarely before an equal. The word occurs over 170 times in the Hebrew Bible, most often of prayer. It is used most often of worshipping God, but sometimes it describes idol worship. In ancient times, a person would fall down before someone who possessed a higher status. People would bow before a king to express complete submission to his rule. Following the example of the ancient people of faith, true Christian worship must express more than love for God; it must also express submission to His will. [1]

How can we keep our worship of the Lord focused on Him and pleasing to Him?

Sing! Sing! Sing! Do you enjoy singing to the Lord? Alone? With others? What songs best express your heart for the Lord and why?

The best conclusion to our lesson today will be to worship the Lord with His word. Please read the beloved Psalm 100 and let it be your guide to worshipping the Lord as the King who reigns on high!

Psalm 100 ^{NAS}

A PSALM FOR THANKSGIVING.

¹ Shout joyfully to the LORD, all the earth.
² Serve the LORD with gladness;
Come before Him with joyful singing.
³ Know that the LORD Himself is God;
It is He who has made us, and not we ourselves;
We are His people and the sheep of His pasture.

⁴ Enter His gates with thanksgiving
And His courts with praise.
Give thanks to Him, bless His name.
⁵ For the LORD is good;
His lovingkindness is everlasting
And His faithfulness to all generations.

Arranging the Flowers

Psalm 101

It is so very hard not to pick each and every psalm for our study! Psalm 101 is attributed to David and reflects his dedication to live his life according to God's ways and His word. The previous psalms have described the love and justice of our God the King, and this psalm pictures that same character of uprightness and goodness in the heart of David the king. "I will sing of lovingkindness and justice, to You, O Lord, I will sing praises. I will give heed to the blameless way. I will walk within my house in the integrity of my heart." (Psalm 101:1-2 ^{NAS}) David's song of praise to the Lord is a life of personal integrity.

Psalm 102

Following the psalm of David, we find a "prayer of the afflicted when he is faint and pours out his complaint before the Lord." (Psalm 102: heading) In the midst of Book Four, where the Lord is praised as the King who reigns on high, we see from Psalm 102 that the Israelites are in exile and suffering. This psalmist recognizes that their suffering was because of the wrath of the Lord: "For I have eaten ashes like bread and mingled my drink with weeping because of Your indignation and Your wrath, for You have lifted me up and cast me away…" (Ps. 102:9-10 ^{NAS}), but he also recognizes that his hope is in the Lord: "You will arise and have compassion to Zion; for it is time to be gracious to her, for the appointed time has come." (Ps. 102:13 ^{NAS}) In their grief they are learning to trust that the Lord is faithful.

Psalms 103 – 106

The last four psalms of Book Four follow the "prayer of the afflicted" with declarations of praise to the Lord for His many blessings. A modern worship chorus says: "Why so downcast O my soul? Put your hope in God – and bless the Lord O my soul." That's what we seem to find here following the suffering of Psalm 102. Psalm 103 blesses the Lord for all of His benefits to His people.

Psalm 104 blesses the Lord for His splendor and His care of creation. Psalm 105 blesses the Lord by giving Him thanks for His wonderful works on behalf of the nation of Israel, from His covenant with Abraham through His care of Joseph, to His redemption of the nation out of Egypt and into the Promised Land. Psalm 106 blesses the Lord, praising Him for His lovingkindess and patience with His people's rebellion.

Psalm One Hundred and Three

Let us bless the Lord with all our heart, soul, mind and strength. Psalm 103 is a favorite, well-known, beautiful psalm that captures many precious truths about our God and the benefits of our relationship with Him. In the springtime, bright yellow daffodils pop up from the dreary winter beds and bring a smile to my face. God's benefits to us are far greater than any pretty little flower and should brighten our faces even in dismal circumstances.

Please read Psalm 103.

Respond with your reflections, questions, prayers or praise.

_____

_____

_____

_____

The flow of thought, the structure, and the key points of this psalm stand out a little more in the Hebrew than they do in English. We can certainly understand the message just as it is written, but I'd like you to see an overview of the psalm before we go any further.

Very briefly, summarize each verse and look at the overall thought pattern.

Psalm 103

1   Bless the Lord!

     Bless His holy name!

2   Bless the Lord!

     Forget none of His benefits!

3   He is the one who: _____

     He is the one who: _____

4   He is the one who: _____

     He is the one who: _____

5   He is the one who: _____

6   He is the one who: _____

7   He has: _____

8   He is: _____

9   He will not: _____

10 He has not: _____

11 Because: _____

12 Because: _____

13 Because: _____

14 Because: _____

15 Mankind is the one who: _____

16 Because: _____

17 But the Lord is the one who: _____

     to those who: _____

18   to those who: _____

     to those who: _____

19 The Lord: _____

20 Bless the Lord! …all you who: _____

21 Bless the Lord! … all you who: _____

22 Bless the Lord! … all: _____

     Bless the Lord O my soul!

I once asked a friend what biblical, spiritual word she would like to be used to describe her life and character. After a very brief pause, she answered: "I'd like to be known as a thankful person." I was amazed, delighted, and challenged by her answer. In order to have a thankful heart, we must be humble before the Lord recognizing how we deserve nothing; we must be submissive to His will and recognize His sovereignty; we must realize the incredible blessings we have received.

Would you describe yourself as a thankful person? Why or why not?

Please look up the definition of the following word:
Bless: Strong's # 1288
Hebrew word:
Hebrew definition:

This psalm shows us so many reasons to bless the Lord and to give Him thanks. Based on the overview above, which of God's actions toward us is most emphasized?

There are two words that are repeated throughout this psalm that tell us about the Lord's character that prompts His actions. We've looked up one of them before, but it's time for a review!

Please look up the definition for the following words:
Compassion (v.4)/ compassionate (v.8) / have compassion (v. 13):
  each derived from Strong's # 7355
Hebrew word:
Hebrew definition:

Lovingkindness (v. 4, v. 8, v. 11, v. 17): Strong's #2617
Hebrew word:
Hebrew definition:

David remembered and believed what the Lord said about Himself and what Moses taught him. What do the following verses say?

Exodus 20:5-6

Exodus 34:6-8

Deuteronomy 7:9

Punishment or pardon - which do you deserve?

We undeniably deserve punishment for our sins. But – as far as the east is from the west, so far has He removed our transgressions from us. Superlatives are in order here! Only the most extravagant images can begin to express how God treats sin and sinners. Bless the Lord O my soul! All that is within me, bless His holy name! Psalm 103 emphasizes the incredible forgiveness that the Lord gives us based on His mercy, love, grace and patience.

> There is too much in the Psalm for a thousand pens to write, it is one of those all-comprehending Scriptures which is a Bible in itself, and it might alone almost suffice for the hymn-book of the church. [2]

It's important to notice that the Lord is specific about who will receive the benefits of His grace. "The lovingkindness of the Lord is from everlasting to everlasting on those who fear Him." (Psalm 103:17 [NAS], also in verses 11, 13)

What do those who fear the Lord do according to Psalm 103:18?

The psalm concludes with instructions to the angels and all servants of the Lord to bless Him. He is the King on the throne (Psalm 103:19), worthy of all adoration, thanks, and submission. A New Testament complement to this psalm is found in Ephesians 1. Paul sums it up well saying: "Blessed be the God and Father of our Lord Jesus Christ, who has blessed us with every spiritual blessing in the heavenly places in Christ" (Eph. 1:3 [NAS]). Oh yes – let us bless the Lord!

Bless the LORD, O my soul!
O LORD my God, You are very great
You are clothed with splendor and majesty
Psalm 104:1 [NKJ]

Oh give thanks to the LORD, call upon His name;
Make known His deeds among the peoples.
Sing to Him, sing praises to Him;
Speak of all His wonders.
Psalm 105:1 – 2 [NAS]

Praise the LORD!
Oh give thanks to the LORD, for He is good;
For His lovingkindness is everlasting.
Psalm 106:1 [NAS]

The Conclusion of Book Four: Psalms 105 and 106

As we come to the end of Book Four, we should remember the despair of Book Three. The Israelites were devastated because of the destruction of the city of Jerusalem, the temple of the Lord, and the throne of David. They were left without a king and wanted to know "O God, why have You rejected us forever?" (Psalm 74:1) The psalms found in Book Four show that Israel realized that the Lord Himself was their King – forever. And they show that He will be faithful to His covenant.

*Psalm 105 rehearses God's great acts in creating and delivering a nation for Himself. The point of the psalm is to instruct the people to **remember** what He has done on their behalf. Remembering His incredible works in the past should give them hope for the future.*

Please read through the psalm below and notice the summaries of the historical events that I've given you. The dividing lines should help to outline the different periods over 500 years in Israel's history. It's important to read through this psalm to notice God's goodness before we read Psalm 106 which reviews Israel's rebellion.

Psalm 105 [NAS]

1   Oh give thanks to the LORD, call upon His name;
    Make known His deeds among the peoples.
2   Sing to Him, sing praises to Him;
    Speak of all His wonders.

3   Glory in His holy name;
    Let the heart of those who seek the LORD be glad.
4   Seek the LORD and His strength;
    Seek His face continually.
5   Remember His wonders which He has done,
    His marvels and the judgments uttered by His mouth,
6   O seed of Abraham, His servant,
    O sons of Jacob, His chosen ones!

The instructions here are to give thanks and praise the Lord because of the wonderful works He did on behalf of Israel. The seed of Abraham and sons of Jacob are to **remember** what the Lord did in the history of their nation.

7   He is the LORD our God;
    His judgments are in all the earth.
8   He has remembered His covenant forever,
    The word which He commanded to a thousand generations,
9   The covenant which He made with Abraham,
    And His oath to Isaac.
10 Then He confirmed it to Jacob for a statute,
    To Israel as an everlasting covenant,
11 Saying, "To you I will give the land of Canaan
    As the portion of your inheritance,"

Everlasting Covenant with Patriarchs – Abraham, Isaac, Jacob (Gen. 12, 26, 35)

12 When they were only a few men in number,
    Very few, and strangers in it.
13 And they wandered about from nation to nation,
    From one kingdom to another people.
14 He permitted no man to oppress them,
    And He reproved kings for their sakes:
15 "Do not touch My anointed ones,
    And do My prophets no harm."

Abraham wandered from Ur to Haran to Canaan to Egypt (Gen.11 – 12)
God protected him from pharaohs and kings (Gen.12, 20)

16 And He called for a famine upon the land;
    He broke the whole staff of bread.
17 He sent a man before them,
    Joseph, who was sold as a slave.
18 They afflicted his feet with fetters,
    He himself was laid in irons;
19 Until the time that his word came to pass,
    The word of the LORD tested him.
20 The king sent and released him,
    The ruler of peoples, and set him free.

Joseph's brothers sold him as a slave to Potiphar, who then cast him into prison. But then Pharaoh needed his dreams interpreted and sent for Joseph. His God-given interpretation regarding a coming famine gave him respect in Pharaoh's eyes and he was made a ruler second only to Pharaoh. (Gen. 37 – 41)

21 He made him lord of his house
    And ruler over all his possessions,
22 To imprison his princes at will,
    That he might teach his elders wisdom.
23 Israel also came into Egypt;
    Thus Jacob sojourned in the land of Ham.
24 And He caused His people to be very fruitful,
    And made them stronger than their adversaries.
25 He turned their heart to hate His people,
    To deal craftily with His servants.

> Israel (Jacob) and his sons traveled to Egypt under Joseph's care and over 400 years grew into a great nation that Pharaoh came to hate. (Ge. 47, Ex. 1)

26 He sent Moses His servant,
    And Aaron, whom He had chosen.
27 They performed His wondrous acts among them,
    And miracles in the land of Ham.
28 He sent darkness and made it dark;
    And they did not rebel against His words.
29 He turned their waters into blood
    And caused their fish to die.
30 Their land swarmed with frogs
    Even in the chambers of their kings.
31 He spoke, and there came a swarm of flies
    And gnats in all their territory.
32 He gave them hail for rain,
    And flaming fire in their land.
33 He struck down their vines also and their fig trees,
    And shattered the trees of their territory.
34 He spoke, and locusts came,
    And young locusts, even without number,
35 And ate up all vegetation in their land,
    And ate up the fruit of their ground.
36 He also struck down all the firstborn in their land,
    The first fruits of all their vigor.

> God called Moses out of the desert to shepherd the nation of Israel and deliver them out of the hands of the Egyptians. He showed His great power through sending ten plagues. (Ex. 7 – 11)

37 Then He brought them out with silver and gold,
    And among His tribes there was not one who stumbled.
38 Egypt was glad when they departed,
    For the dread of them had fallen upon them.
39 He spread a cloud for a covering,
    And fire to illumine by night.

> Pharaoh commanded them to leave, the Egyptians gave Israel their possessions, and the Lord went before them by cloud and fire. (Ex. 12:31 – 36, 13:18 - 22)

⁴⁰ They asked, and He brought quail,
   And satisfied them with the bread of heaven.
⁴¹ He opened the rock and water flowed out;
   It ran in the dry places like a river.
⁴² For He remembered His holy word
   With Abraham His servant;
⁴³ And He brought forth His people with joy,
   His chosen ones with a joyful shout.
⁴⁴ He gave them also the lands of the nations,
   That they might take possession of the fruit of the peoples' labor,
⁴⁵ So that they might keep His statutes and observe His laws,
   Praise the LORD!

> The Lord provided manna, water, and quail during their journey through the wilderness. He demonstrated that He was faithful to His covenant with Abraham and gave them the land He had promised…. A place where they could serve and obey the Lord.

What mighty, wonderful works has the Lord done in your life that it is important for you to remember?

Now we come to the last psalm of Book Four, which summarizes the failures and rebellions of the nation of Israel. It is one of the longest confessions of sin in the Bible. The placement of this psalm at this point in the book of Psalms shows that the nation realized that the destruction of Jerusalem, the temple, and the kingdom were a result of their sin against God. It ends with a plea for His deliverance and restoration.

Please read through this psalm and highlight or mark the confessions of the sins of the Israelites in one color, and the character and actions of the Lord in another color.

Psalm 106 ᴺᴬˢ

¹ Praise the LORD!
   Oh give thanks to the LORD, for He is good;
   For His lovingkindness is everlasting.
² Who can speak of the mighty deeds of the LORD,
   Or can show forth all His praise?
³ How blessed are those who keep justice,
   Who practice righteousness at all times!

⁴ Remember me, O LORD, in Your favor toward Your people;
   Visit me with Your salvation,
⁵ That I may see the prosperity of Your chosen ones,
   That I may rejoice in the gladness of Your nation,

That I may glory with Your inheritance.

6 We have sinned like our fathers,
We have committed iniquity, we have behaved wickedly.

7 Our fathers in Egypt did not understand Your wonders;
They did not remember Your abundant kindnesses,
But rebelled by the sea, at the Red Sea.

8 Nevertheless He saved them for the sake of His name,
That He might make His power known.

9 Thus He rebuked the Red Sea and it dried up,
And He led them through the deeps, as through the wilderness.

10 So He saved them from the hand of the one who hated them,
And redeemed them from the hand of the enemy.

11 The waters covered their adversaries;
Not one of them was left.

12 Then they believed His words;
They sang His praise.

13 They quickly forgot His works;
They did not wait for His counsel,

14 But craved intensely in the wilderness,
And tempted God in the desert.

15 So He gave them their request,
But sent a wasting disease among them.

16 When they became envious of Moses in the camp,
And of Aaron, the holy one of the LORD,

17 The earth opened and swallowed up Dathan,
And engulfed the company of Abiram.

18 And a fire blazed up in their company;
The flame consumed the wicked.

19 They made a calf in Horeb
And worshiped a molten image.

20 Thus they exchanged their glory
For the image of an ox that eats grass.

21 They forgot God their Savior,
Who had done great things in Egypt,

22 Wonders in the land of Ham
And awesome things by the Red Sea.

23 Therefore He said that He would destroy them,
Had not Moses His chosen one stood in the breach before Him,
To turn away His wrath from destroying them.

24 Then they despised the pleasant land;
They did not believe in His word,

²⁵ But grumbled in their tents;
They did not listen to the voice of the LORD.
²⁶ Therefore He swore to them
That He would cast them down in the wilderness,
²⁷ And that He would cast their seed among the nations
And scatter them in the lands.

²⁸ They joined themselves also to Baal-peor,
And ate sacrifices offered to the dead.
²⁹ Thus they provoked Him to anger with their deeds,
And the plague broke out among them.
³⁰ Then Phinehas stood up and interposed,
And so the plague was stayed.
³¹ And it was reckoned to him for righteousness,
To all generations forever.

³² They also provoked Him to wrath at the waters of Meribah,
So that it went hard with Moses on their account;
³³ Because they were rebellious against His Spirit,
He spoke rashly with his lips.

³⁴ They did not destroy the peoples,
As the LORD commanded them,
³⁵ But they mingled with the nations
And learned their practices,
³⁶ And served their idols,
Which became a snare to them.
³⁷ They even sacrificed their sons and their daughters to the demons,
³⁸ And shed innocent blood,
The blood of their sons and their daughters,
Whom they sacrificed to the idols of Canaan;
And the land was polluted with the blood.
³⁹ Thus they became unclean in their practices,
And played the harlot in their deeds.

⁴⁰ Therefore the anger of the LORD was kindled against His people
And He abhorred His inheritance.
⁴¹ Then He gave them into the hand of the nations,
And those who hated them ruled over them.
⁴² Their enemies also oppressed them,
And they were subdued under their power.
⁴³ Many times He would deliver them;
They, however, were rebellious in their counsel,
And so sank down in their iniquity.

⁴⁴ Nevertheless He looked upon their distress
When He heard their cry;
⁴⁵ And He remembered His covenant for their sake,
And relented according to the greatness of His lovingkindness.
⁴⁶ He also made them objects of compassion
In the presence of all their captors.

⁴⁷ Save us, O LORD our God,
And gather us from among the nations,
To give thanks to Your holy name
And glory in Your praise.
⁴⁸ Blessed be the LORD, the God of Israel,
From everlasting even to everlasting.
And let all the people say, "Amen."
Praise the LORD!

This psalm confesses these sins:

Rebellion	Discontent	Ingratitude	Forgetting God
Idolatry	Unbelief	Arrogance	Compromise
Envy	Disobedience		

Based on who God is and how He treated His people, was there any reason for these sins?

Please examine your life – based on who God is and how He treats you, is there any reason for you to commit these sins? Is there anything you need to confess to the Lord?

Please look once more at Psalm 106:1-5 and 47-48, and fill in the blanks below:

Psalm 106:1 _____ _____ _____!

Psalm 106:4 _____ _____, O Lord, in Your favor toward Your people;

Visit me with Your _____

Psalm 106: 47 _____ _____, O Lord our God,

And gather us from among the nations, to give thanks to Your holy name
And glory in Your praise.

Psalm 106:48 Blessed be the Lord, the _____ _____ _____,
From everlasting even to everlasting. And let all the people say, "Amen."

_____ ____ _____!

What does Israel realize they need? Based on Psalm 106, why do they need it?

Psalm 106 is a "hallelujah" psalm, beginning and ending with this imperative of praise, translated in the NIV as "Praise the LORD." In comparison, while Psalm 105 ends with "Praise the LORD," it does not begin with the imperative. Psalms 105 and 106, therefore, were an appropriate reappraisal of the covenant at a time when Israel's hope had failed. These poems propound the thesis that even though Israel had broken the covenant, Yahweh was faithfully compassionate. Relying upon that compassion, ***another historical miracle was yet possible.*** Just as he had heard their cry in Egypt (Ex. 3:7), He was still listening in this new era of national distress.[1] [emphasis added]

Book Five: Psalms 107 — 150
Introduction

Another historical miracle was yet possible! Do you believe it? The Lord isn't finished with Israel – or you or me – yet! The best is yet to come, and we will all give thanks to His holy name and glory in His praise! The psalms of Book Five will keep our hope alive and our eyes looking to the Lord who reigns on high.

Arranging the Flowers

Psalm 107

A wonderful refrain echos throughout this psalm – a call to give thanks to the Lord for His lovingkindness. This opening line and repeated verse (v. 8, 15, 21, 31) connect it to Psalm 106 so that Book Four and Book Five are woven together. This psalm is also another rehearsal of the history of Israel and God's goodness to them, "bringing them out of their distresses" over and over again. The last line gives the intent of the whole psalm, saying: "Who is wise? Let him give heed to these things, and consider the lovingkindnesses of the Lord." (Psalm 107:43[NAS]) This historical, wisdom psalm prompts the reader to maintain hope that "another historical miracle was yet possible!"

Psalm 108

And now a few words from – David. He was a wise king who knew that when he cried for help, the Lord would answer and deliver because of His lovingkindness (Ps.107). So this psalm exalts the Lord and shows confidence in Him. "Be exalted, O God, above the heavens, and Your glory above all the earth. That Your beloved may be delivered, save with Your right hand, and answer me!" (Ps. 108:5-6 [NAS]) This psalm also included a few words from – God. He declares that He will be victorious over Israel's enemies. This psalm shows the faith of one who knows that God must be the one to deliver: "Oh give us help against the adversary, for deliverance by man is in vain. Through God we will do valiantly, and it is He who shall tread down our adversaries." (Psalm 108:12-13[NAS])

Psalm 109

David is once again an example of one who turns to God during times of acute distress, in this psalm, at the hands of a wicked slanderer. This psalm is an emotional, aggressive prayer for the Lord to execute justice against David's enemy. "Let his days be few, let another take his office." (Ps. 109:8 [NAS]) This verse was quoted by Peter (Acts 1:20) and applied to Judas, who had become the accuser and betrayer of Jesus.

Psalm One Hundred and Ten

It's time for a short psalm that packs a powerful prophetic proclamation! It will keep us looking to the future with the hope of the reign of the Messiah. After two psalms that mentioned God's justice over the enemies of His people, this psalm also encourages Israel and us that God has a plan. The most potent, pungent little flower that I know of is the bright and sturdy marigold, planted in gardens for bold color and to keep the insect pests away. Here is a golden psalm proclaiming the deity, majesty, and priesthood of the One to come who will overcome the kings of the earth.

Please read Psalm 110.

Respond with your reflections, questions, prayers or praise.

_____

_____

_____

_____

One of the things we have to look forward to in our study of this psalm is the commentary that Jesus Himself gives us about Psalm 110, and the many references to it in the New Testament. But we will start with the seven verses recorded by David.

Who is speaking to whom in verse 1? Do you remember the Hebrew words for the names of the Lord? (See page 122)

A little word here that we take for granted is actually very important in the interpretation of this psalm. Look up the definition for:

Says: Strong's #5002
Hebrew word:
Hebrew definition:

The same word is used 21 times in Isaiah, 158 times in Jeremiah and 85 times in Ezekiel. In the old King James Version, it's often translated as "thus saith the LORD". This word is used throughout the Scriptures to indicate divine announcements.

So, the use of this word in this psalm means what?

What is the specific divine announcement in verse 1?

Now look at Psalm 110:2 and 3. These statements are not made in 1st person ("I"), but in 3rd person. David is speaking now to his Lord. How does Psalm 110:2 relate to Psalm 2:4-9?

The following verses were the earliest prophecies of the Messiah's rule over His enemies. What do you learn from them?
Genesis 49:10

Numbers 24:17-18

1 Samuel 2:10

What is being emphasized about the Messiah in Psalm 110:1-3 and 5-7?

Psalm 110:4 indicates another divine announcement, although "na-hoom" isn't used in this verse. The language used is very strong though – it shows that God has made an irrevocable decree. The structure of the psalm indicates that this decree was made from Yahweh to the Messiah, just as in verse 1.

What has God sworn to that He will not change His mind about?

This verse is quoted five times in Hebrews! (Heb. 5:6; 5:10; 6:20; 7:17; 7:21) It's an extremely important point.

Please note what you learn about Melchizedek's name and priesthood, and about the Messiah's priesthood according to:
Hebrews 6:19 – 7:3

Hebrews 7:21-25

Please note what you learn about the Messiah from the prophecy in Zechariah 6:12-13.

How would you summarize the message of Psalm 110?

Let's look now at what Jesus wanted the people to realize from this psalm. Please read Matthew 22:41-46. Remember that "Christ" is the Greek word for "Anointed," which in Hebrew is "Mashiach" – Messiah.

Who did the Pharisees say the Messiah would be?

What do we learn about David's utterance of Psalm 110?

What does Jesus indicate about the Messiah in Matthew 22:43?

What is the point of Jesus' question in Matthew 22:45?

...since David was the highest ruler in the kingdom, his *Adonai* had to be the Lord Himself. It was this fact that Jesus presented to the Pharisees, asking them how David's Lord could also be David's son (Messiah). The only answer is *by incarnation*: the eternal Son of God had to come to earth as a human born into the family of David. [1]

Please look at one more reference to this psalm. It will bring it all together for us and show us the application for our lives. Peter preached a great sermon on the day of Pentecost. We'll join in for his closing comments.

Please read Acts 2:32-39.
Who is Jesus according to Acts 2:36? (Don't forget what "Christ" means.)

What did that realization cause for those who heard the message?

Have you realized that Jesus is, as we have seen according to Psalm 110, Lord, High Priest, and Conquering King? Have you realized that He is the Messiah? Are these more than names and titles to you? What impact do these roles of Jesus have on you?

Jesus Christ is the One now seated at the right hand of God the Father. Every New Testament reference to that position is based on Psalm 110:1! The prophecy of Christ's exaltation and priesthood has been fulfilled. And the day is coming when He will return to earth and crush His enemies.

"Jesus said to him, '...hereafter you will see
THE SON OF MAN SITTING AT THE RIGHT HAND OF POWER, and COMING ON
THE CLOUDS OF HEAVEN.' "
Matthew 26:64 [NAS]

Until that day, let us hope in Him, honor Him, confess to Him, and submit to Him. He is our High-Priest King on High.

Arranging the Flowers

I'd like to summarize Psalms 107 – 117 with just a short phrase for each one that I hope will give you a bird's eye view of the forest. Then we'll get back to looking at the flowers again!

Psalm 107 – an historical poem that shows that God delivered from oppression in the past and He can deliver again

> "Then they cried out to the Lord in their trouble;
> He delivered them out of their distresses." Psalm 107:6 NAS

Psalm 108 – a cry for deliverance from oppression

> "Save with Your right hand, and answer me!" Psalm 108:6 NAS

Psalm 109 – a cry for vengeance against those oppressing

> "Let my accusers be clothed with dishonor, And let them cover themselves with
> their own shame as with a robe." Psalm 109:29 NAS

Psalm 110 – a statement from God that He will crush His King's enemies (deliverance) and make His King a priest

> "Sit at my right hand
> until I make Your enemies a footstool for Your feet." Psalm 110:1 NAS

Psalm 111 – a declaration of praise because God is faithful to His covenant

> "He has ordained His covenant forever;
> Holy and awesome is His name." Psalm 111:9 NAS

Psalm 112 – a declaration of praise because God is faithful to the righteous

> "Light arises in the darkness for the upright;
> He is gracious and compassionate and righteous." Psalm 112:4 NAS

Psalm 113 – a declaration of praise because God exalts the lowly

> "He raises the poor from the dust
> And lifts the needy from the ash heap." Psalm 113:7 NAS

Psalm 114 – a remembrance of God's deliverance of Israel from Egypt

> "Tremble, O earth, before the Lord,
> Before the God of Jacob,
> Who turned the rock into a pool of water,
> The flint into a fountain of water." Psalm 114:7-8 NAS

Psalm 115 – an exhortation to trust in the Lord

> "O Israel, trust in the Lord;
> He is their help and shield.
> O house of Aaron, trust in the Lord
> He is their help and shield.
> You who fear the Lord, trust in the Lord;
> He is their help and their shield." Psalm 115:9-11 [NAS]

Psalm 116 – a testimony of the deliverance of the Lord

> "The Lord preserves the simple;
> I was brought low, and he saved me." Psalm 116:6 [NAS]

Psalm 117 – the shortest psalm, which is an exhortation for all nations to praise the Lord for His lovingkindness

> "Praise the LORD, all nations;
> Laud Him, all peoples!
> For His lovingkindness is great toward us,
> And the truth of the LORD is everlasting.
> Praise the LORD!" Psalm 117:1-2 [NAS]

Why do you think these psalms have been placed together?

These psalms paint a picture of hope for Israel. In the midst of their present trials, they can remember God's mighty works in the past, cry out to Him for help, and know that He will be faithful to His word and deliver them. When He does save them, all nations around the world will praise Him.

Have you heard of The Egyptian Hallel? That is the title given to Psalms 113 – 118. The Israelites recited these psalms on several festival occasions, including Passover, the Feast of Weeks (Pentecost), the Feast of Tabernacles, The Feast of Dedication (Hanukah) and the New Moon festival. It's called the Egyptian Hallel because "hallel" means praise, and these psalms rejoice in God's deliverance of His people out of Egypt. The Levites would have chanted it verse by verse before the altar at the Temple when the Passover lambs were being slain and families chanted it in their homes at their Passover Feast.

There is a general consensus that this group of psalms was the "hymn" that Jesus sang at the conclusion of the Last Supper (His Passover feast). The last psalm of this group, Psalm 118, praises the Lord and prophesies of the suffering and exaltation of Christ.

Psalm One Hundred and Eighteen

Please read Psalm 118.

Respond with your reflections, questions, prayers or praise.

_____

_____

_____

_____

It's been a long time since we've mentioned the poetic device called "inclusio." The first and the last lines are the same, indicating the theme of the poem. This psalm repeats its major theme in verse 1 and verse 29 emphasizing an attribute of the Lord.

What is the main theme of Psalm 118?

What in the psalm gives evidence of this theme? Record phrases below. Make sure you notice an important word (it's repeated three times).

You have probably already noticed several familiar verses and have realized that this psalm is quoted in the New Testament. It is filled with hope for the Messiah to be the One who comes in the name of the Lord to save the people. Let's spend some time looking at how this psalm was spoken by and applied to Jesus.

O LORD, do save, we beseech You;
O LORD, we beseech You, do send prosperity!
Blessed is the one who comes in the name of the LORD;
We have blessed you from the house of the LORD.
Psalm 118:25-26 ^{NAS}

What was the reason that Jesus quoted from this verse in Luke 13:34-35?

What was the occasion and why was this verse quoted in Matthew 21:1-11?

Hosanna! This word is the Greek transliteration of the Hebrew "hoshi-ah na" in Psalm 118:25 and it means "please save us!"

Please look up the following words:
Save: Strong's #3467
Hebrew word:
Hebrew definition:

Salvation: Strong's #3444
Hebrew word:
Hebrew definition:

Jesus:

Strong's Greek#2424	**Strong's Hebrew #3091**
Greek word:	**Hebrew word:**
Greek definition:	**Hebrew definition:**

Do you see the connection between the words save, salvation and Jesus? What is it?

Why did the crowd cry out for salvation? The accounts above don't show the reason that the Israelite crowd cried out for salvation, but history tells us that they wanted freedom from foreign oppression. At the time of Christ, the Romans were ruling over the land and the people. Just as Psalm 118 described, Israel was surrounded by enemies. They were looking for their Messiah to deliver them from other nations and return their national identity to them once again.

Have you cried out to be saved? From what?

How do the following verses explain why we need salvation?
Romans 2:5-6

Galatians 3:10

Ephesians 2:1-2, 12

Jesus' last days in Jerusalem provided salvation for all who would ask Him for it. A few days after Jesus' triumphal entry into Jerusalem, He told a parable and quoted this psalm. He understood the reason that God had sent Him to earth.

Please read Matthew 21:33-45.
In the parable, what happened to the son of the landowner?

What will happen to the vinedressers?

What is the correlation between the parable and the quote from Psalm 118:22? Who is the stone? Who are the builders?

How are you responding to the Son of God? Is there anything about Him that you are rejecting? His authority? His instructions?

After Jesus' death and resurrection, Peter came to understand what he had been taught and he declared the truth of who Jesus was to the Sanhedrin when he was arrested.

Please read Acts 4:5-12.
Who does Peter say is "the stone which was rejected"?

Who does Peter say rejected the stone?

What is the correlation between Psalm 118:21-26 and Acts 4:12?

We observed earlier that the theme of Psalm 118 was the goodness and lovingkindness of God. The New Testament authors realized that God's character was intricately related to salvation.

Please read Titus 3:4-7.
What does this verse tell you about the reason God has given salvation?

What does this verse tell you about how God gives salvation?

Receiving Christ involves turning to God from self (this is called repentance) and trusting Christ to come into our lives to forgive our sins and to make us what He wants us to be. Just to agree intellectually that Jesus Christ is the Son of God and that He died on the cross for our sins is not enough. Nor is it enough to have an emotional experience. We receive Jesus Christ by faith.

You Can Receive Christ Right Now by Faith Through Prayer:

Lord Jesus, I need You to save me. Thank You for dying on the cross for my sins. I surrender my life to you and receive You as my Savior and Lord. Thank You for forgiving my sins and giving me eternal life. Take control of the throne of my life. Make me the kind of person You want me to be.

Please turn back to Psalm 118:23-24. What was the psalmist's response to the statement made in verse 22?

Is the salvation of the Lord through Jesus Christ's death and resurrection "marvelous in your eyes?" How is it "the Lord's doing?"

What else can we say except: "Give thanks to the Lord, for He is good: For His lovingkindness is everlasting." Praise the Lord. Hallelujah. Jesus saves.

Psalm One Hundred and Nineteen

Here we are. At the longest psalm in the Psalter. At the longest chapter in the Bible. At a poem which is longer than thirty individual books of the Bible! Before beginning my study of Psalm 119, I was familiar with its theme. I knew that it reflected on the Word of God, His commands, His laws, His ways. But I thought that because every line of this poem referred to the Word of God, it would be repetitive. I thought this psalm would just say the same thing over and over again. It doesn't!

This psalm is like the field of flowers on the cover of our workbook – we'll be looking at the same "species" of flower – but the field is full of many colors, and there is much that is communicated through this poem. This is good news! This psalm is simple enough to understand without doing great research and cross-referencing. We will spend our time in this lesson reading and absorbing what the author has expressed in this masterpiece of poetry.

At this point in our lesson, I normally ask you to read the psalm in its entirety. It's not quite time for that yet. I want you to see the structure of this psalm. It has 22 stanzas – or sections, corresponding to the 22 letters of the Hebrew alphabet. Each stanza is eight lines long, and each line begins with the same letter of the alphabet appropriate to that stanza. One commentator has called this "a holy alphabet for Zion's scholars."

Here's the Hebrew alphabet:

aleph	א	waw	ו	kaf	כ	ayin	ע	shin	שׁ
bet	ב	tzayin	ז	lamed	ל	pe	פ	tav	ת
gimel	ג	khet	ח	mem	מ	tsade	צ		
dalet	ד	tet	ט	nun	נ	qof	ק		
he	ה	yod	י	samek	ס	resh	ר		

Your Bibles may have the appropriate Hebrew letter and its name above the corresponding stanzas.

What you will see on the next page will probably seem very strange, but the beauty of this psalm can be captured just by looking at it in the original Hebrew language. You don't have to know Hebrew! Just look at the first letter of each line on the far right! (Hebrew is written from right to left... to illustrate with English letters – the word **psalms** would be: **smlasp.**

Highlight the first word, or letter of each stanza. Use four different colors – one for verses 1 – 8, one for verses 9 – 16, one for verses 17 – 24, and one for verses 25 – 32.

Start here:

$\longrightarrow$

1 אַשְׁרֵי תְמִימֵי־דָרֶךְ הַהֹלְכִים בְּתוֹרַת יְהֹוָה

2 אַשְׁרֵי נֹצְרֵי עֵדֹתָיו בְּכָל־לֵב יִדְרְשׁוּהוּ

3 אַף לֹא־פָעֲלוּ עַוְלָה בִּדְרָכָיו הָלָכוּ

4 אַתָּה צִוִּיתָה פִקֻּדֶיךָ לִשְׁמֹר מְאֹד

5 אַחֲלַי יִכֹּנוּ דְרָכָי לִשְׁמֹר חֻקֶּיךָ

6 אָז לֹא־אֵבוֹשׁ בְּהַבִּיטִי אֶל־כָּל־מִצְוֹתֶיךָ

7 אוֹדְךָ בְּיֹשֶׁר לֵבָב בְּלָמְדִי מִשְׁפְּטֵי צִדְקֶךָ

8 אֶת־חֻקֶּיךָ אֶשְׁמֹר אַל־תַּעַזְבֵנִי עַד־מְאֹד

9 בַּמֶּה יְזַכֶּה־נַּעַר אֶת־אָרְחוֹ לִשְׁמֹר כִּדְבָרֶךָ

10 בְּכָל־לִבִּי דְרַשְׁתִּיךָ אַל־תַּשְׁגֵּנִי מִמִּצְוֹתֶיךָ

11 בְּלִבִּי צָפַנְתִּי אִמְרָתֶךָ לְמַעַן לֹא אֶחֱטָא־לָךְ

12 בָּרוּךְ אַתָּה יְהֹוָה לַמְּדֵנִי חֻקֶּיךָ

13 בִּשְׂפָתַי סִפַּרְתִּי כֹּל מִשְׁפְּטֵי־פִיךָ

14 בְּדֶרֶךְ עֵדְוֹתֶיךָ שַׂשְׂתִּי כְּעַל כָּל־הוֹן

15 בְּפִקֻּדֶיךָ אָשִׂיחָה וְאַבִּיטָה אֹרְחֹתֶיךָ

16 בְּחֻקֹּתֶיךָ אֶשְׁתַּעֲשָׁע לֹא אֶשְׁכַּח דְּבָרֶךָ

17 גְּמֹל עַל־עַבְדְּךָ אֶחְיֶה וְאֶשְׁמְרָה דְבָרֶךָ

18 גַּל־עֵינַי וְאַבִּיטָה נִפְלָאוֹת מִתּוֹרָתֶךָ

19 גֵּר אָנֹכִי בָאָרֶץ אַל־תַּסְתֵּר מִמֶּנִּי מִצְוֹתֶיךָ

20 גָּרְסָה נַפְשִׁי לְתַאֲבָה אֶל־מִשְׁפָּטֶיךָ בְכָל־עֵת

21 גָּעַרְתָּ זֵדִים אֲרוּרִים הַשֹּׁגִים מִמִּצְוֹתֶיךָ

22 גַּל מֵעָלַי חֶרְפָּה וָבוּז כִּי עֵדֹתֶיךָ נָצָרְתִּי

23 גַּם יָשְׁבוּ שָׂרִים בִּי נִדְבָּרוּ עַבְדְּךָ יָשִׂיחַ בְּחֻקֶּיךָ

24 גַּם־עֵדֹתֶיךָ שַׁעֲשֻׁעָי אַנְשֵׁי עֲצָתִי

25 דָּבְקָה לֶעָפָר נַפְשִׁי חַיֵּנִי כִּדְבָרֶךָ

26 דְּרָכַי סִפַּרְתִּי וַתַּעֲנֵנִי לַמְּדֵנִי חֻקֶּיךָ

27 דֶּרֶךְ־פִּקּוּדֶיךָ הֲבִינֵנִי וְאָשִׂיחָה בְּנִפְלְאוֹתֶיךָ

28 דָּלְפָה נַפְשִׁי מִתּוּגָה קַיְּמֵנִי כִּדְבָרֶךָ

29 דֶּרֶךְ־שֶׁקֶר הָסֵר מִמֶּנִּי וְתוֹרָתְךָ חָנֵּנִי

30 דֶּרֶךְ־אֱמוּנָה בָחָרְתִּי מִשְׁפָּטֶיךָ שִׁוִּיתִי

31 דָּבַקְתִּי בְעֵדְוֹתֶיךָ יְהוָה אַל־תְּבִישֵׁנִי

32 דֶּרֶךְ־מִצְוֹתֶיךָ אָרוּץ כִּי תַרְחִיב לִבִּי

I know you don't know what these letters mean, but, I hope this visual aid will give you a sense of the incredible skill that the author of this poem applied to his love of the word of God. All 22 stanzas of this psalm reflect his devotion, dedication, and discipline concerning the Scriptures.

One other very important thing to point out about this psalm is that the author used eight different words for the Scriptures. They are listed below. He directly mentions Scripture with one of these words in all but seven out of the 176 verses of this psalm. If we highlighted the repeated words in this psalm, almost every verse would have a word highlighted!

> *Law (in Hebrew: Torah) – referring to all of God's instruction*
> *Testimony*
> *Precept*
> *Statute*
> *Commandment*
> *Judgment (or ordinance) – in the sense of a "rule for living"*
> *Word (of God)*
> *Promise*

We looked up several of these words in our two previous studies on "Torah" psalms. Look back at Psalm 1 and Psalm 19 for reminders of their meanings. It is possible that the author of this psalm was reflecting on both of these earlier psalms when he penned this poem.

Now let's read it in English and start to grasp the message of the psalm.

Please read Psalm 119 – in its entirety.

Respond with your reflections, questions, prayers or praise.

_____

_____

_____

_____

Have you ever read this psalm in its entirety before? Did anything surprise you as you read it?

What surprised me was that this psalm is not a dry, monotone description of God's word. Instead, it is a passionate expression of dedication to the Lord and His ways. Commentators have noted that this psalm contains cries of lament, expressions of trust, prayers of thanksgiving, and statements of wisdom.

> The language of Psalm 119 is the language of devotional poetry: the outpouring of the most intense religious feeling. [1]

Please read through Psalm 119 again, and notice how often the psalmist is desperate for the Lord to intervene in his life – whether through teaching him His commands, or comforting him, or delivering him from his enemies. You may want to highlight, or mark with an arrow or asterisk, each verse that is a prayer request.

What are some of his requests that express the desire of your heart?

Why is the psalmist so passionate about God's word? He expresses his understanding of the blessing that comes from knowing, believing, and obeying all that the Lord has spoken. **Please read through this psalm again** and note a few of the promises and blessings that come from delighting in the Word of God.

> "If your law had not been my delight, I would have perished in my affliction." (Psalm 119:92) Martin Luther wrote this verse in his own hand on his Bible. The date was 1542, with much of his reforming work behind him, and only four years before his death in 1546. [2]

Have you noticed how much of this psalm refers to the affliction that the author has experienced? He repeatedly asks the Lord to revive him – according to His word.

What does the very last verse of this psalm indicate?

With this in mind, please read Psalm 119:65-80. What did the psalmist learn from his affliction? Who brought it upon him?

Is this, therefore, a psalm of a petrified slave cowering before a cruel master? No! What do the following verses emphasize?

Psalm 119:76

Psalm 119:88

Psalm 119:124

Psalm 119:149

Psalm 119:159

Do you remember that the lovingkindness of the Lord, His "chesed", is the foundation of His covenant with Abraham, Israel, and David? This psalm focusing on the word of the Lord was not placed in the book of Psalms without a plan. It's placement right here continues to keep our focus on trusting the Lord, through His word, until the Messiah returns, and His covenant is fulfilled. Much earlier in this study, I pointed out that there are three "Torah" psalms (Psalms 1, 19, 119), and each of them is followed by Messianic psalms. Hmmm. That means that we should soon see psalms that point to the Messiah. We will.

I haven't asked you too many questions in the lesson today, but I did ask you to read and reread this incredible poem focusing on the necessity and sufficiency of Scripture.

Has your time in Psalm 119 convicted, challenged or confirmed you regarding your attitude, aptitude, or obedience to His word?

> There is no book like the Bible. It is a miracle of literature, a perennial spring of wisdom, a wonderful book of surprises, a revelation of mystery, an infallible guide of conduct, an unspeakable source of comfort. [3]

<u>Now it's time for a creative, though-provoking exercise.</u> The author of Psalm 119 probably spent a lot of time composing this masterpiece. Why don't you spend some time, as he did, capturing your thoughts and prayers regarding God's word – from A to Z?

The Songs of Ascents
Psalms 120 — 134

Following all three "Torah" psalms (Psalms 1, 19, and 119) there are Messianic psalms. This arrangement by the compiler directs us to realize that trusting in the Word of God and trusting in the Son of God is the way to live a life which is pleasing to God and which is rewarding to us.

Psalm 2 is a Messianic psalm which prophecies of God anointing His Son as King. Psalms 22, 23, and 24 prophesy of the death, resurrection, and return of the Son of God. And Psalms 120 through 134 are considered a group of Messianic psalms because they focus on (1) the return of the Israelites to Jerusalem, (2) the priority of the temple, and (3) the Davidic king – the Messiah.

Psalms 120 through 134 must be seen as a group because each one of them has the same title: *A Song of Ascents.* Most of these fifteen psalms are short, have various themes, and present a kaleidoscope of images. But their identical titles link them together, and even in their diversity, we can find common themes which then lead us to understand their Messianic outlook.

There are several different perspectives on how this particular group of psalms was used in the lives of the Israelites. One view is that exiles returning from Babylon to Jerusalem sang them. Another view is that they were sung each year when the Israelite families would make their pilgrimage to Jerusalem for the annual festivals of Passover, the Feast of Weeks, and the Feast of Tabernacles. (This is the most widely accepted understanding.) One additional perspective is that in later times, the Levites would sing these fifteen psalms as they climbed the fifteen steps of the temple. Passages from the Mishnah (a written record of the oral law of Judaism) and the Tosefta (a supplement to the Mishnah) indicate this.

It's interesting to think about *how* and *when* these psalms were sung, but for our study, it is more important to examine *where* and *why* these psalms were placed in the psalter as they are. The title here is a critical piece of information. Songs of Ascents are about "going up" in some way. Scholars who have extensively studied these psalms have divided them in three groups of five:

Psalm 120	Psalm 125	Psalm 130
Psalm 121	Psalm 126	Psalm 131
Psalm 122	Psalm 127	Psalm 132
Psalm 123	Psalm 128	Psalm 133
Psalm 124	Psalm 129	Psalm 134

Circle the central psalm in each division above.

Please read Psalm 122. What place is the focus of this psalm, with its name repeated three times? Note this next to the psalm in the chart.

Please read Psalm 127. Who is recognized as the author of this psalm? What did he build? (Remember also that the Lord promised David a "house": a dynasty, through his children.) Note this next to the psalm in the chart.

Please read Psalm 132. What promise to David is repeated in this psalm? Note this next to the psalm in the chart.

> With the different emphases of these center psalms, one gets a "coherent theological view" that points to Zion as the place of blessing where Israel should "go up", a kind of second exodus. [1]

The following words and phrases are repeated throughout these psalms:

"who made the heavens and the earth" – Psalm 121:2; 124:8, 134:3

"both now and forevermore" – Psalm 121:8; 125:2; 131:3

"peace" – Psalm 120:7; 122:6; 125:5; 128:6

"May the Lord bless you from Zion" – Psalm 128:5; 124:3

"O Israel, put your hope in the Lord" – Psalm 130:7; 131:3

If you consider the three central psalms noted above and their focus, plus the repeated phrases above, what is the overall impact of these psalms? I see a community longing for the reign of their perfect King from His temple in Jerusalem. I see a group who is hoping in the Lord and trusting that He will bless them. I see faithful followers of the Lord pressing onward and upward through the difficulties of life on earth until they see their King! That's an example that we can follow!

Arranging the Flowers

Psalm 135
This psalm is a response to the call to praise at the end of the Songs of Ascents which says: "Bless the Lord, all servants of the Lord...!" (Psalm 134:1 [NAS]) And so – Psalm 135 begins "Praise the Lord! Praise Him, O servants of the Lord..." and goes on to recount the greatness of God from the time of creation, through the exodus from Egypt, and in the conquering of Canaan. The call to praise the Lord continues in the last verse and leads us into the next psalm.

Psalm 136

"Give thanks to the Lord for He is good, for His lovingkindness is everlasting."
Psalm 136:1 [NAS]

There should be no doubt by the end of this psalm that "His lovingkindness is everlasting"! It is the refrain echoing after each statement about God's character and goodness. The reading of this psalm should be exciting. Read it with your family! Let your children shout out the refrain. Don't hold back and don't get bored. The truth of this psalm will carry you through the deepest, darkest shadows and give you hope in your own battles.

Psalm 137

This psalm captures the despair and grief experienced by the exiles in Babylon.
"By the rivers of Babylon there we sat down and wept, when we remembered Zion."
Psalm 137:1 [NAS]

Sorrow is real and does not have to be ignored or stuffed away. This psalm shows how to express it to the Lord, remembering who He is, and trusting Him to make things right. Some see this psalm as a "matching bookend" to Psalm 120 which began the Songs of Ascents. Even though the return from Babylonian exile did not initiate the promised Messianic Kingdom, it did indicate that God was still at work and had not abandoned His people or His promise.

Psalm 138

Of David! The next eight psalms are by the beloved shepherd-songwriter. And then the book of Psalms will come to a grand and glorious close with what seems like a thousand hallelujahs. But there is trouble before the end comes, and David once again gives us an example of trusting the Lord:

"Though I walk in the midst of trouble, You will revive me; You will stretch forth
Your hand against the wrath of my enemies, and Your right hand will save me.
The Lord will accomplish what concerns me; Your lovingkindness, O Lord, is
everlasting; do not forsake the works of Your hands."
Psalm 138:7-8 [NAS]

Psalm One Hundred and Thirty-Nine

There are only a few more flowers to be picked for our bouquet. There are so many exquisite blooms, it's hard to say that one is the most beautiful of them all. But Psalm 139 does stand out as a radiant specimen, like a bright pink, sweet smelling stargazer lily. Reading this psalm is like eavesdropping on an intimate expression of adoration and trust from David to the Lord. While some may be afraid at how well the Lord knows them and therefore they fear His judgment, David instead takes comfort in the truth of the closeness of God.

Please read Psalm 139.

Respond with your reflections, questions, prayers or praise.

_____

_____

_____

_____

What is your favorite, or most meaningful, verse from this psalm? Why?

David expresses his understanding of God's nature and then responds to that truth. He speaks from personal experience and from his understanding of God's word. There are echoes of the wisdom of Job found in this psalm.

We describe God as "omniscient" – all-knowing. David explains this attribute to us beautifully in verses 1-6. What does he say God knows? Pay attention to the repetition of the word "know".

How do the following verses express the truths seen in verse 6?
Job 42:3

Romans 11:33

Please look up the definition for the following word:
Wonderful - Strong's #6383
Hebrew word:
Hebrew definition:

How does your own knowledge and understanding compare to that of God's? What does this mean about your capacity to comprehend God's ways? What is your reaction to this?

We also describe God as "omnipresent" – He is "everywhere present." David describes this attribute in verses 7-12. Where does he say God is?

Are you curious about God's presence in Sheol (NIV: depths)? What does that mean? Let's look at a few other verses that mention something similar. What do you learn from:

Job 26:6

Proverbs 15:11

Jeremiah 23:24

> While Sheol is not within Yahweh's sphere of blessing, it is within the sphere of divine sovereignty. [1]

What is the benefit of God's omnipresence according to Psalm 139:7-12?

In this psalm, David presents us with a paradox… Psalm 139:2 [NAS] *says: "You understand my thought from afar" and Psalm 139:7* [NAS] *says: "where can I flee from Your presence?" God is far off and near. He is transcendent and intimate. We cannot reconcile these truths about our great God, we can only bow our heads and hearts in wonder and awe.*

Another of God's incredible attributes is that He is "omnipotent" – all-powerful. David reflects on this truth in verses 13-18. What does he say God has done? How is God's power described regarding David's life on earth?

Do you praise God for the work of His hands and the creation of your life?

Job experienced extreme trials that made him regret the day of his birth, but he did recognize that he was God's workmanship.

What does Job 10:10-11 say?

Isaiah 44:24 declares the mind-boggling truth about our omnipotent God as well. What does he say?

Does the truth of Ecclesiastes 11:5 comfort you or concern you?

"How precious are Your thoughts to me, O God! How vast is the sum of them! If I should count them, they would outnumber the sand. When I awake, I am still with You." David reacts to his understanding of God's personal involvement in his life with thanksgiving and praise. He recognizes that the great I am is his Lord, his God, and while intimately involved in his life, He is still incomprehensible.

Because David knows that God is involved in his life, he pleads for His intervention in verses 19-24. Commentators see this section of the psalm as describing God's holiness and His vengeance. How are these two attributes reflected in these verses?

Please read through Psalm 139 in its entirety again. Meditate on the overwhelming, indescribable, infinity of the Lord as you do so.

What is your response to Him?

Please look up the definition for the following word:
Search – Strong's #2713
Hebrew word:
Hebrew definition:

Note what is said in Psalm 139:1 and 23.

We cannot hide from the Lord. And He is best worshipped when we bow before His holiness and open ourselves willingly to His penetrating gaze. He looks upon us with love that will purify us and lead us in the everlasting way. Are you willing to pray as David did and as Spurgeon did below?

> Exercise any and every test upon me. By fire and by water let me be examined. Read not alone the desires of my heart, but the fugitive thoughts of my head. Know with all-penetrating knowledge all that is or has been in the chambers of my mind. What a mercy that there is one being who can know us to perfection! He is intimately at home with us. He is graciously inclined towards us, and is willing to bend His omniscience to serve the end of our sanctification. Let us pray as David did, and let us be as honest as he. [2]

We are about to begin the grand finale of praise to our God. I hope you're ready. Psalm 139 has appropriately magnified the Lord and minimized ourselves.

Arranging the Flowers

Psalm 140

"Rescue me, O Lord, from evil men..."
Psalm 140:1 [NAS]

The plea for help in Psalm 139 is echoed by David again, as is his confidence that the Lord is will show Himself faithful. David knows that God is "the strength of his salvation" and that He has "covered his head in the day of battle." Psalm 140:7 David is still an example of a righteous man leaving judgment of the wicked in God's hands.

Psalm 141

David expresses through this psalm that he has once again been treated unjustly by evil men. And once again, David is an example of one who waits on the Lord to carry out His justice. While he waits, he prays:

"Set a guard, O Lord, over my mouth; keep watch over the door of my lips.
Do not incline my heart to any evil thing..."
Psalm 141:3-4 [NAS]

Psalm 142

"I cry aloud with my voice to the Lord.... I pour out my complaint before Him..."
Psalm 142:1-2 [NAS]

Troubles will come even to the godly. As the book of Psalms comes to a close, the editor seems to emphasize, by placing these cries for help one after the other, that David persevered through the trials of his life by crying out to the Lord and trusting Him.

Psalms 143 and 144

There are three more psalms of David. I'd like you to read Psalm 143 and 144, with the included commentaries, and then we will begin our study of the everlasting hallelujahs to our God, Savior, and King.

Psalm 143 [NAS]

A PSALM OF DAVID.

1 Hear my prayer, O LORD,
Give ear to my supplications!
Answer me in Your faithfulness, in Your righteousness!
2 And do not enter into judgment with Your servant,
For in Your sight no man living is righteous.
3 For the enemy has persecuted my soul;
He has crushed my life to the ground;
He has made me dwell in dark places, like those who have long been dead.

⁴ Therefore my spirit is overwhelmed within me;
My heart is appalled within me.

⁵ I remember the days of old;
I meditate on all Your doings;
I muse on the work of Your hands.
⁶ I stretch out my hands to You;
My soul longs for You, as a parched land.
Selah.

⁷ Answer me quickly, O LORD, my spirit fails;
Do not hide Your face from me,
Or I will become like those who go down to the pit.
⁸ Let me hear Your lovingkindness in the morning;
For I trust in You;
Teach me the way in which I should walk;
For to You I lift up my soul.
⁹ Deliver me, O LORD, from my enemies;
I take refuge in You.

¹⁰ Teach me to do Your will,
For You are my God;
Let Your good Spirit lead me on level ground.
¹¹ For the sake of Your name, O LORD, revive me.
In Your righteousness bring my soul out of trouble.
¹² And in Your lovingkindness, cut off my enemies
And destroy all those who afflict my soul,
For I am Your servant.

Though essentially the same in content and general theme as the preceding psalms of David in this section of the book (140 – 142), this psalm adds significantly to the overall message of Psalms. It first of all adds the dimension of seeking God's will amid trials and troubles. Here David not only laments his troubles, but he also meditates on God's Word, seeking to understand His ways (v.5). In this respect, the psalm is similar to the introductory psalm (Ps.1), where the counsel is given to meditate on God's Word day and night as the means of finding success and blessing in this life.

Second, this psalm adds the notion of God's leading by His Spirit (v.10). Throughout the Scriptures we are taught that the godly must depend on God's Spirit for guidance, wisdom, and strength. In this psalm, David is presented as a model of such dependence. The concepts presented here are clearly those of the new covenant (cf.Eze.36:2; Rom. 8:4). [1]

Psalm 144 ^{NAS}

A PSALM OF DAVID.

¹ Blessed be the LORD, my rock,
Who trains my hands for war,
And my fingers for battle;
² My lovingkindness and my fortress,
My stronghold and my deliverer,
My shield and He in whom I take refuge,
Who subdues my people under me.
³ O LORD, what is man, that You take knowledge of him?
Or the son of man, that You think of him?
⁴ Man is like a mere breath;
His days are like a passing shadow.

⁵ Bow Your heavens, O LORD, and come down;
Touch the mountains, that they may smoke.
⁶ Flash forth lightning and scatter them;
Send out Your arrows and confuse them.
⁷ Stretch forth Your hand from on high;
Rescue me and deliver me out of great waters,
Out of the hand of aliens
⁸ Whose mouths speak deceit,
And whose right hand is a right hand of falsehood.

⁹ I will sing a new song to You, O God;
Upon a harp of ten strings I will sing praises to You,
¹⁰ Who gives salvation to kings,
Who rescues David His servant from the evil sword.
¹¹ Rescue me and deliver me out of the hand of aliens,
Whose mouth speaks deceit
And whose right hand is a right hand of falsehood.

¹² Let our sons in their youth be as grown-up plants,
And our daughters as corner pillars fashioned as for a palace;
¹³ Let our garners be full, furnishing every kind of produce,
And our flocks bring forth thousands and ten thousands in our fields;
¹⁴ Let our cattle bear
Without mishap and without loss,
Let there be no outcry in our streets!
¹⁵ How blessed are the people who are so situated;
How blessed are the people whose God is the LORD!

Continuing in the same vein as the preceding Davidic psalms (140 – 143), David now calls on the Lord to come to the rescue of the righteous. In the imagery used here by David, however, a new dimension is given to his prayers. There is a clear note of immanency sounded in this psalm, coupled with a widening of his vision of God's intervention. David prays that God would "part the heavens… and come down; touch the mountains, so that they smoke" (v.5). Elsewhere in the Scriptures such language is usually reserved for the descriptions of the Lord's victorious coming at the end of the ages (cf. Dan 7:14; Hab 3:3-6).

In light of the fact that the book of Psalms has increasingly focused the reader's attention to the imminent hope of the coming of the Lord, it seems likely that the composer sees in David's poetic imagery an expression of the same hope. He intends for us to draw the conclusion that David himself shared the hope of the Lord's glorious and victorious return. Certainly the picture David paints at the close of this psalm shows that he expected God's intervention on his behalf to do more than to restore normalcy. He expected the Lord's return to establish a kingdom of peace and prosperity unequaled by anything Israel had yet experienced (144:12-15).[1]

Psalm One Hundred and Forty-Five

Are you ready for the return of the Lord? Come, let us worship Him now, practicing our songs as we anticipate His arrival!

What does Psalm 144:9-10 say?

This is the prelude to the grand finale of praise! New songs, many songs, songs from everything on earth are going to resound throughout the heavens as we worship our King. Psalm 145 is a new song, unlike any that David has ever sung before.

Please read Psalm 145.

Respond with your reflections, questions, prayers or praise.

_____

_____

_____

_____

I believe this psalm is one of David's greatest legacies. It is his most beautiful utterance and the sincere expression of adoration and devotion from one who truly was a man after God's own heart.

What is the title given for this psalm?

Please look up the following word and its root word:

Praise: Strong's #8416   **from root word: Strong's #1984**
Hebrew word: **Hebrew word:**
Hebrew definition: **Hebrew definition:**

This is the only psalm in all of the 150 recorded for eternity which bears this title, specifically being a song of praise! The term "tehillah" was deemed so special and excellent that it was taken from this psalm and given to the whole collection – entitled by the Jews as "sefer tehillim" – Book of Praises.

Psalm 145 is an acrostic, which as we have mentioned previously, is a form of poetry using the alphabet as a guide. This type of poetry is used to focus on one particular theme, and the theme of this psalm is God's greatness as King.

To whom does David address this praise in Psalm 145:1?

What does he plan to do according to verses 1-2?

This psalm of great praise is full of action. List the words and verbs that indicate what David and the people will do in their adoration of the King.
For example: v.1 – I will extol You, I will bless Your name

How often and how long will David and the people praise the Lord?

How often do you praise the Lord?

Because David focused his attention on the attributes and actions of God, we will do the same. He says: "Great is the Lord, and highly to be praised, and His greatness is unsearchable" (v. 3). While the word "great" in the Hebrew Scriptures was as common an adjective as it is in our own language, it still "most often describes the size or the magnitude of the word it modifies." [1] As David uses this word to honor God, he is obviously aware that we don't even begin to know or understand how great He is – he says "His greatness is unsearchable", which indicates that it is impossible to comprehend. It is conceivable that this song of praise is David's attempt at "searching out" the greatness of God, knowing full well he will never succeed.

What attributes and actions of God are praised in the following verses?
Psalm 145:4

Psalm 145:5

Psalm 145:7

Psalm 145:8

Psalm 145:9-10

Psalm 145:13

Psalm 145:14-17

Psalm 145:18

Psalm 145:19-20

In my studies on some of the words used in this psalm to describe the Lord, I found some information that I would like to share with you. The words David uses in verse 5 as he meditates on God have been translated in the NAS as "the glorious splendor of your majesty". One beautiful word is piled upon another, even in our language. But the words in Hebrew convey so much more than we grasp in English. This phrase could be translated: "the splendor of the glory of your majesty". The first word –"splendor" – is most frequently applied in the Scriptures to the king and his royal majesty.

The second word used is one of the most immense words applied to God - "kabod" glory. While His "greatness" (v. 3) is unsearchable, His "glory" is unfathomable. The basic meaning of the root of this word is "to be heavy, weighty," and from this we get the concept of a "weighty" person, someone who is honorable, impressive, worthy of respect.

In Psalm 145, "glory" is used to refer to the dignity, wealth, and high position of God. David uses this word three times in his song of praise. David was fully aware that the glory of the Lord eclipsed the glory of any earthly king.

The third word David uses is "hod" which can be translated as splendor, majesty, vigor, glory, or honor. The phrase "the glorious splendor of Your majesty" shows us that one word alone cannot fully express the stunning nature of the Lord.

Keeping in mind that this psalm is praise to the King, we should take note of how His kingdom is described? What do you learn from verses 11-13?

The next verses (14-20) describe what a good King the Lord is to His people. You've listed already listed these attributes and actions. But please notice that there is a qualification given regarding who He will hear and to whom He will respond.

What is necessary in the lives of the people of the Lord according to Psalm 145:18-20?

What are we reminded of in verse 20 regarding those who do not submit to the Lord?

Please return to the beginning of this book of praises and read the prophetic wisdom given in Psalm 2.

Based on Psalm 2, who is the King of Psalm 145?

What has sustained the authors of the psalms throughout all their trials? The Word of God. What have they anticipated and prayed for repeatedly? The fulfillment of His covenant with David and the kingdom of the Messiah. What have they asked God to remember? His "chesed" – faithful, loyal love.

At the close of the book of Psalms, the editor has placed a psalm of David's in which the focus is on the eternal reign of God the King. The whole of the book of Psalms has been geared toward the recognition of the Son of God as the anointed King who will one day reign on earth and who will reign for eternity.

And the end of the book celebrates the truth that the Lord is the King at this moment, and is the King for eternity. What else can we do but praise Him with hallelujahs?!

What does Psalm 145:21 say?

In our next lesson, we'll join the chorus that is already resounding in the heavens by reading the incredible doxology found in Psalm 146 through 150.

The Doxology
Psalms 146 – 150

Praise the Lord! Hallelujah! Did you know that "hallelujah" is an accurate transliteration of the Hebrew? When you say "hallelujah", you are actually speaking a Hebrew command which means: "all of you, praise Yahweh!" The word is an imperative command. It's time to follow that exciting exhortation and let our hearts sing out with praise to our great God, to His Son the King, who is our Savior.

Come, let us worship!

Please read Psalm 146.

Respond with your reflections, questions, prayers or praise.

_____

_____

_____

_____

Please read Psalm 147.

Respond with your reflections, questions, prayers or praise.

_____

_____

_____

_____

Please read Psalm 148.

Respond with your reflections, questions, prayers or praise.

_____

_____

_____

_____

Please read Psalm 149.

Respond with your reflections, questions, prayers or praise.

_____

_____

_____

_____

Please read Psalm 150.

Respond with your reflections, questions, prayers or praise.

_____

_____

_____

_____

We've looked at all the "flowers" of this book, and our bouquet is complete. It is extravagant with blooms that reflect magnificent truths, amazing prophecies, abundant compassion in trials, and strong, steadfast faith. In our study of the psalms, I feel like I have journeyed through the life of David, through his trials and triumphs, and I feel like I have journeyed through the history of Israel with its trials and triumphs as well.

My own life has paralled the ups and downs, the praises and prayers, the hopes and hallelujahs of the psalms. I am more convinced than ever that our God is a great and mighty, loving, compassionate, faithful God with a plan! He is the only one in whom to trust and He will see me through whatever this life on earth may bring. His lovingkindness is better than life. Hallelujah. Praise the Lord. He is my God and Savior.

Please write your own hallelujah to the Lord. It can be based on one of the Doxology Psalms (146—150).

Hallelujah!
(based on Psalm 150)

Praise the Lord!
Once again... and forevermore...
Hallelujah!

Praise God – He is in His sanctuary
His glory has returned to the temple

Praise God in His mighty expanse
No temple can contain Him

Praise Him for His mighty deeds
They have been displayed and He has rescued us

Praise Him according to His excellent greatness
He is Holy
He is Worthy
He is Righteous
He is Wise
He is Sovereign
He is Powerful
He is Faithful
He is Gracious
He is Loving

Praise God with
Trumpet sounds!
And harp!
And lyre!
And timbrel!
And dancing!
And strings!
And pipe!
And loud cymbals!
And resounding cymbals!

Let everything that has breath praise the Lord
Hallelujah!

Let all words – all celebration – all sounds
Be directed to Yahweh
Our God
Our King
Our Savior
Hallelujah!
Amen and Amen.

COME, LET US WORSHIP

Endnotes

Psalm 15
1. Rogerson, J. W., and J.W. McKay. *Psalms.* Vol. 1, *Psalms 1-50.* Cambridge Commentary on the New English Bible. (Cambridge: Cambridge University Press, 1977).
2. Goldingay,John. *Psalms.* Vol. 1, *Psalms 1-42.* Baker Commentary on the Old Testament, Wisdom and Psalms, edited by Tremper Longman III. (Grand Rapids: Baker Academic, 2006), 222.

Psalm 17
1. Bullock, C. Hassell, *Encountering the Book of Psalms.* (Grand Rapids: Baker Academic, 2001), 166.
2. C. H. Spurgeon, The Treasury of David, Vol. 1a, Psalms 1-26 (Grand Rapids: Zondervan, 1968), 215.

Psalm 18
1. Goldingay, *Psalms,* 251.
2. Barnes, Albert, *Albert Barnes Notes on the Bible,* www.e-sword.net, Ps 18:1.
3. Bromily, Geoffrey William, *International Standard Bible Encyclopedia,* (Grand Rapids: Eerdmans, 1979), horn.
4. Spurgeon, *The Treasury of David, 239.*

Psalm 19
1. Boice, James Montgomery, *Psalms.* Vol. 1, *Psalms 1—41.* (Grand Rapids: Baker, 2005), 171.
2. C. S. Lewis, *Reflections on the Psalms* (New York: Harcourt, Brace and World, 1958), 63.
3. Sailhammer, John H., *NIV Compact Bible Commentary.* (Grand Rapids, Zondervan, 1994), 319.

Psalm 22
1. Lawson, Steven J. , *Psalms 1-75,* Holman Old Testament Commentary, edited by Max Anders. (Nashville, Broadman and Holman, 2003), 114.

Psalm 27
1. Craigie, Peter C. *Psalms 1-50,* Word Biblical Commentary, vol. 19. (Waco: Word, 1983), 231.
2. Craigie, *Psalms 1-50,* 232.
3. Harris, R. Laird, Gleason L. Archer, Jr., and Bruce K. Waltke. *Theological Wordbook of the Old Testament,* 2 vols. (Chicago: Moody Press, 1980), temple.
4. Passion, *Give Me One Pure and Holy Passion,* Sparrow Records.

Psalm 29
1. Keil, C.F.; F. Delitzsch, *Keil and Delitzsch Commentary on the Old Testament,* www. E-sword.net, Ps. 29:6.

Psalm 31
1. The NET Bible, New English Translation, Copyright 2005 by Biblical Studies Press, L.L.C., www.bible.org, Ps. 31:9, note #16.

Psalm 32
1. Lawson, *Psalms 1-75,* Ps. 32.
2. Morris, Leon, *The Biblical Doctrine of Judgment,* (London: Tyndale Press, 1960).

Psalm 33
1. Craigie, *Psalms 1-50.*

Psalm 34
1. Goldingay, *Psalms,* 478.
2. The NET Bible, Ps.34:22.

Psalm 37
1. Agapeland: Music Machine, *Have Patience,* Birdwing Records, 1977.
2. VanGemeren, W., ed. *New International Dictionary of Old Testament Theology and Exegesis,* (Grand Rapids: Zondervan, 1986), delight.
3. Spurgeon, *The Treasury of David, 239.*
4. Spurgeon, *The Treasury of David,* Ps. 37.

Psalms 42-49
1. Sailhammer, *NIV Compact Bible Commentary,* 323.

Psalm 50
1. Goldingay,John. *Psalms.* Vol. 2, *Psalms 42-89.* Baker Commentary on the Old Testament, Wisdom and Psalms, edited by Tremper Longman III. (Grand Rapids: Baker Academic, 2006),112.
2. Wilson, Gerald H., *Psalms Volume 1,* The NIV Application Commentary, (Grand Rapids: Zondervan, 2002), 762.
3. http://www.brainyquote.com/quotes/quotes/a/aristotle141386.html, 08/11/2008.

Psalm 51
1. Wiersbe, Warren. *Expository Outlines of the Old Testament.* Quickverse.

Psalm 61
1. Bromily, Geoffrey William, *International Standard Bible Encyclopedia*, wings.
2. Wilson, Gerald H., *Psalms Volume 1,* 873.

Psalm 63
1. Spurgeon, *The Treasury of David,* Ps. 63.

Psalm 68
1. Tate, Marvin E. *Psalms 51-100.* Word Biblical Commentary, (Waco: Word, 1990), 170.
2. Lawson, *Psalms 1-75,* 338.
3. Tate, *Psalms 51-100,* 180-181.
4. Hobbs, Al. *So You Would Know,* Brooklyn Tabernacle Choir, High and Lifted Up, Warner Bros. Records, (Hobeal Publishing SESAC, 1997).

Psalm 69
1. Lawson, *Psalms 1-75,* 346.

Psalm 71
1. Clarke, Adam and Ralph Earl, *Adam Clarke's Commentary on the Bible, (*Grand Rapids: Baker, 1967), Ps. 71.
2. Clarke, *Adam Clarke's Commentary on the Bible,* Ps. 71.
3. http://www.quotationspage.com/quotes/Abigail_van_Buren

Psalm 72
1. Lawson, *Psalms 1-75,* 358.

Psalms 73-76
1. Lawson, *Psalms 1-75,* 365

Psalms 84-89
1. Tate, *Psalms 51-100,* 350.
2. Theological Dictionary of the Old Testament, sabaoth, Bibleworks.

Psalm 90
1. Wiersbe, Warren. *Be Exultant Psalms 90-150,* (Colorado Springs: Cook Communications, 2004), 14.

Psalms 93-99
1. Lawson, Steven J. , *Psalms 76-150,* Holman Old Testament Commentary, edited by Max Anders. (Nashville, Broadman and Holman, 2006), 114.

Psalm 103
1. Keil, C.F.; F. Delitzsch, *Keil and Delitzsch Commentary on the Old Testament,* Ps. 103:1.
2. Spurgeon, C.H., *The Treasury of David,* Vol. 2, Psalms 58-110, (Grand Rapids: Zondervan, 1968), 275.

Psalm 105-106
1. Bullock, *Encountering the Book of Psalms,* 68.

Psalm 110
1. Wiersbe, *Be Exultant,* 74.

Psalm 119
1. Allen, Leslie C. *Psalms 101-150,* Word Biblical Commentary, (Waco: Word, 1983), 185.
2. Bullock, *Encountering the Book of Psalms,* 220.
3. Lawson, *Psalms 76-150,* 251.

Psalms 120-134
1. Bullock, *Encountering the Book of Psalms,* 80.

Psalm 139
1. Allen, *Psalms 101-150, 329.*
2. Spurgeon, C.H., *The Treasury of David,* Vol. 23, Psalms 111-150, (Grand Rapids: Zondervan, 1968), 266.

Psalm 143
1. Sailhammer, *NIV Compact Bible Commentary,* 347.

Psalm 144
1. Sailhammer, *NIV Compact Bible Commentary,* 347

Psalm 145
1. VanGemeren, *New International Dictionary of Old Testament Theology and Exegesis,* "great".

Suggested Resources

The Complete Word Study Dictionary by Spiros Zhodiates

The Strongest Strong's Exhaustive Concordance by James Strong — available through online resources below and Google

Suggested (free) online study helps:
These include various Bible translations and links to all resources mentioned below.

studylight.org   **searchgodsword.org**   **blueletterbible.org**

e-sword.net (free program to download, then available offline)

The following list includes study helps that are available for free online if you are interested in pursuing more information about the Scriptures on your own. Descriptions are from e-sword.net.

Commentaries:

Robertson's Word Pictures in the New Testament
Robertson's magnum opus has a reputation as one of the best New Testament word study sets. Providing verse-by-verse commentary, it stresses meaningful and pictorial nuances implicit in the Greek but often lost in translation. And for those who do not know Greek, exegetical material and interpretive insights are directly connected with studies in the original text. All Greek words are transliterated.

Treasury of Scriptural Knowledge
This classic Bible study help gives you a concordance, chain-reference system, topical Bible and commentary all in one! Turn to any Bible passage, and you'll find chapter synopses, key word cross-references, topical references, parallel passages and illustrative notes that show how the Bible comments on itself. This really is a treasure!

Vincent's Word Studies
Marvin Vincent's Word Studies has been treasured by generations of pastors and laypeople. Commenting on the meaning, derivation, and uses of significant Greek words and idioms, Vincent helps you incorporate the riches of the New Testament in your sermons or personal study without spending hours on tedious language work!

John Gill's Exposition of the Entire Bible
Having preached in the same church as C. H. Spurgeon, John Gill is little known, but his works contain gems of information found nowhere outside of the ancient Jewish writings. John Gill presents a verse-by-verse exposition of the entire Bible.

Jamieson, Fausset and Brown Commentary

Long considered one of the best conservative commentaries on the entire Bible, the JFB Bible Commentary offers practical insight from a reformed evangelical perspective. The comments are an insightful balance between learning and devotion, with an emphasis on allowing the text to speak for itself.

Keil & Delitzsch Commentary on the Old Testament

This commentary is a classic in conservative biblical scholarship! Beginning with the nature and format of the Old Testament, this evangelical commentary examines historical and literary aspects of the text, as well as grammatical and philological issues. Hebrew words and grammar are used, but usually in content, so you can follow the train of thought.

Dictionaries:

Easton's Bible Dictionary

Easton's Bible Dictionary provides informative explanations of histories, people and customs of the Bible. An excellent and readily understandable source of information for the student and layperson. This dictionary is one of Matthew George Easton's most significant literary achievements.

International Standard Bible Encyclopedia

This authoritative reference dictionary explains every significant word in the Bible and Apocrypha! Learn about archaeological discoveries, the language and literature of Bible lands, customs, family life, occupations, and the historical and religious environments of Bible people.

Smith's Bible Dictionary

A classic reference, this comprehensive Bible dictionary gives you thousands of easy-to-understand definitions, verse references and provides a wealth of basic background information that you'll find indispensable as you read the Bible.

Thayer's Greek Definitions

For over a century, Joseph Henry Thayer's Greek-English Lexicon of the New Testament has been lauded as one of the finest available! Based on the acclaimed German lexicon by C.L.W. Grimm, Thayer's work adds comprehensive extra-biblical citations and etymological information, expanded references to other works, increased analysis of textual variations, and discussion of New Testament synonyms. An invaluable resource for students of New Testament Greek!

Noah Webster's Dictionary of American English

Noah Webster once wrote, "Education is useless without the Bible." That's why his first dictionary is the only one available today that defines every word in the original language and its biblical usage. Compare Webster's definitions of words like "marriage" and "education" with those found in modern dictionaries, and see the difference for yourself!

Prayer Requests and Praises

Today's Date:

My personal request:

Confidential requests from my friends:

Be joyful always; pray continually; give thanks in all circumstances,
for this is God's will for you in Christ Jesus.
1 Thessalonians 5:16-18 NIV

Prayer Requests and Praises

Today's Date:

My personal request:

Confidential requests from my friends:

Let us therefore come boldly to the throne of grace,
that we may obtain mercy and find grace to help in time of need.
Hebrews 4:16

Prayer Requests and Praises

Today's Date:

My personal request:

Confidential requests from my friends:

I pray that out of His glorious riches
He may strengthen you with power through His Spirit in your inner being.
Ephesians 3:16 NIV

Prayer Requests and Praises

Today's Date:

My personal request:

Confidential requests from my friends:

We can be confident that He will listen to us whenever we ask Him for anything
in line with His will and . . . we can be sure that He will give us what we ask for.
1 John 5:14-15 NLT

Prayer Requests and Praises

Today's Date:

My personal request:

Confidential requests from my friends:

Let us come before His presence with thanksgiving:
and let us shout joyfully to Him with psalms.
Psalms 95:2

Prayer Requests and Praises

Today's Date:

My personal request:

Confidential requests from my friends:

Then you will call upon Me and come and pray to Me, and I will listen to you.
Jeremiah 29:12 (BOA)

Prayer Requests and Praises

Today's Date:

My personal request:

Confidential requests from my friends:

...the Spirit Himself makes intercession for us with groanings which cannot be uttered.
Romans 8:26

Prayer Requests and Praises

Today's Date:

My personal request:

Confidential requests from my friends:

Until now you have not asked for anything in My name.
Ask and you will receive, and your joy will be complete.
John 16:24

Prayer Requests and Praises

Today's Date:

My personal request:

Confidential requests from my friends:

Then Jesus told His disciples a parable
to show them that they should always pray and not give up.
Luke 18:1

Prayer Requests and Praises

Today's Date:

My personal request:

Confidential requests from my friends:

Jesus looked at them and said,
"With man this is impossible, but not with God; all things are possible with God. "
Mark 10:27 NIV

Prayer Requests and Praises

Today's Date:

My personal request:

Confidential requests from my friends:

If you abide in Me, and My words abide in you,
ask whatever you wish, and it shall be done for you.
John 15:7 NASB

Prayer Requests and Praises

Today's Date:

My personal request:

Confidential requests from my friends:

You help us by your prayers.
2 Corinthians 1:11 NIV

Prayer Requests and Praises

Today's Date:

My personal request:

Confidential requests from my friends:

I call to God, and the Lord saves me. Evening, morning and noon
I cry out in distress, and He hears my voice.
Psalm 55:16-17 NIV

Prayer Requests and Praises

Today's Date:

My personal request:

Confidential requests from my friends:

Always keep on praying for all the saints.
Ephesians 6:18 NIV

Prayer Requests and Praises

Today's Date:

My personal request:

Confidential requests from my friends:

The God of Israel Himself gives strength and power to the people.
Psalm 68:35 NAS

Prayer Requests and Praises

Today's Date:

My personal request:

Confidential requests from my friends:

My God shall supply all your need according to His riches in glory by Christ Jesus.
Philippians 4:19 KJV

Prayer Requests and Praises

Today's Date:

My personal request:

Confidential requests from my friends:

Trust in the Lord with all your heart and lean not on your own understanding; in all your ways acknowledge Him, and He will make your paths straight.
Proverbs 3:5-6 NIV

Prayer Requests and Praises

Today's Date:

My personal request:

Confidential requests from my friends:

As I was with Moses, so I will be with you; I will never leave you or forsake you.
Joshua 1:5 NIV

Prayer Requests and Praises

Today's Date:

My personal request:

Confidential requests from my friends:

Behold, I am the Lord, the God of all flesh, is there anything too hard me Me?
Jeremiah 32:27 NKJV

Prayer Requests and Praises

Today's Date:

My personal request:

Confidential requests from my friends:

The Lord God is a sun and shield; The Lord will give grace and glory; No good thing will He withhold from those who walk uprightly.
Psalm 84:11 NKJV

Prayer Requests and Praises

Today's Date:

My personal request:

Confidential requests from my friends:

The Lord bless you and keep you; The Lord make His face shilne upon you, and be gracious to you; The Lord lift up His countenance upon you and give you peace.
Numbers 6:24-26 NKJV

Prayer Requests and Praises

Today's Date:

My personal request:

Confidential requests from my friends:

Dear friend, I pray that you may enjoy good health and that all may go well with you, even as
your sould is getting along well.
3 John 1:2 NIV

Prayer Requests and Praises

Today's Date:

My personal request:

Confidential requests from my friends:

Oh, taste and see that the Lord is good: blessed is the man who trusts in Him!
Psalm 34:8 NKJV

Prayer Requests and Praises

Today's Date:

My personal request:

Confidential requests from my friends:

I will sing to the Lord, because He has dealt bountifully with me
Psalm 13:6 NKJV

OTHER STUDIES BY
ELIZABETH BAGWELL FICKEN

Immeasurably More!: An in-depth study of Ephesians

Do you want your walk with Christ to be more intimate, more faithful, and more obedient? God is able to do immeasurably more than you can imagine through His power in your life! This exciting study will help you understand the never-ending blessings of salvation and the extraordinary potential you have to live a victorious and faithful Christian life.

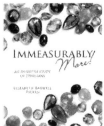

That You May Know the Lord: An in-depth study of Ezekiel

Don't miss this great book! As you study this intriguing prophecy, you will be humbled by the holiness, sovereignty and glory of God; you will be challenged to examine your own lives as you see the sin of the Israelites; you will be inspired as you see the power of the Holy Spirit; and you will be excited as you anticipate wonderful promises to be fulfilled by the Lord.

Follow Me: An in-depth study of the Gospel of Matthew

This study will challenge you to a more passionate commitment to Jesus. Learn from Matthew's eye-witness perspective, his proofs from Old Testament scriptures, and his presentation of Jesus' five sermons, just who Jesus is, what He did, and what He said. Matthew's life was drastically changed from his encounter with Jesus — yours will be too.

Letters to the Thessalonians: An in-depth study of 1st and 2nd Thessalonians

These letters are about faith, hope and love; holiness, prayer, and perseverance; the will of God and the glorious return of Christ. And so much more! Almost every major doctrine of our faith is covered in these personal writings from the apostle Paul. Join me as we read someone else's mail. I'm sure you'll find a few things that you will think were written just to you!

And the Lord Blessed Job: An in-depth study of Job

One of the Lord's blessings to Job was that he was chosen to show Satan that God is worthy of worship no matter what happens in our lives. While the book of Job deals with suffering, it isn't about answering the question "why do people suffer?" It's about humbly submitting to God as the Holy One who is infinite in wisdom, power, justice, and goodness.

Find her! elizabethficken.com or

Available at
amazon.com
and other bookstores